The Nature of Transformation

A comprehensive Life Coaching system inspired by nature to heal your body, mind, and spirit

Janet Zavala

Copyright © 2023 by Janet Zavala

ISBN: 978-1-951131-55-5

Library of Congress Control Number: 9781951131555

Published by As You Wish Publishing
connect@asyouwishpublishing.com
www.asyouwishpublishing.com

All rights reserved.

No portion of this book may be reproduced in any form without written permission from the publisher or author, except as permitted by U.S. Copyright law.

To my dad who focused my gaze on the moon and the stars.
And to my son, who firmly grounded me to Mother Earth.

Contents

Foreword	VII
Introduction	XIII
Section One Preparing for the Journey Ahead	1
Section Two Spring – Discover, Unclutter, Cultivate	55
Section Three Summer – Feed, Nurture, Blossom	107
Section 4 Fall – Harvest, Transform, Preserve	129
Section 5 Winter – Survival, Leveraging Resources, Reorganize	169
Section 6 The Journey Never Ends	203
About the Author	211

Foreword

When I wrote my first middle-grade novel about a 12-year-old fairy with a disability, I had no idea it would ultimately lead me down the path of transformation. I met author and life coach Janet Zavala a few years ago through my wife after learning that we were both drawn to personal development. We listened to the same popular personal development coaches and light workers and together attended a seminar hosted by one of our favorite business and life coaches, Marie Forleo.

Later, Janet and I took a book marketing course together taught by Gabby Bernstein, another famous personal development coach. Upon finishing the course, Janet suggested we create an accountability partnership. At the time, I had this newly published middle-grade novel that I desperately needed to promote and was new to the whole idea of book marketing. I always focused on the actual writing side of creating a novel, but never on the marketing aspect of the writing process and to be honest, it scared me. At the time, Janet's goal was writing a book proposal for this book, *The Nature of Transformation.*

The Nature of Transformation is unique because it uses nature as an inspiring tool along with traditional personal development coaching principles such as gaining clarity and developing a plan to achieve your goals with the help of daily meditation practices, breathwork exercises, and journaling activities.

According to the author, transformation isn't about changing who you are, it's about getting back to your authentic self and who you were before life experiences created fear and doubt within. In the book, there are numerous examples of the way nature transforms and rejuvenates itself with the seasons, and the ways in which this process mirrors that of human transformation. As a nature lover myself, this book affirms what I've instinctively known since childhood. There is a healing vibration in nature's energy. Like my friend and author of this book, I was drawn to the ocean as a teenager and young adult. I would often sneak off to the beach any chance I had because I suffered from anxiety and depression caused by an illness called Meniere's disease, an inner ear disorder that causes severe dizziness, nausea, hearing loss and loss of balance. The amount of school I missed as a child and teenager was immeasurable, which in turn caused a severe lack of confidence and low self-esteem.

Creative writing was the only thing that helped me feel better. I loved the feeling of getting lost in my writing, especially when I was sitting on a sandy shore. Writing and being surrounded by nature has always been a must for my overall well-being, but what I never knew until I read *The Nature of Transformation*, is that my journey to healing and personal development could be taken to the next level. After having read the book and doing the journal exercises, daily meditations and breathwork described in this book, I came to the realization of what had been blocking the success of my own book. Despite the great reviews and positive feedback from my readers, I still wasn't having the type of success that I had envisioned when I first wrote my novel for middle graders. I concluded that my fear of speaking about my book and putting myself out there in the world through media interviews, podcasts, social media, and videos was stemming from the impact Meniere's disease had on me as a child.

My memories of my childhood education are filled with experiences that brought about feelings of failure, being ignored, and bullied by other children as well as teachers due to my constant absences from school. My inability to relate to others at the time made me feel different from others and I didn't know how to talk about how I was feeling.

As a child, I tended to want to disappear and stay small. At the pivotal age of twenty-nine, the symptoms of my illness finally subsided with the proper medical treatment. My goal was now to "catch up in life,". I did what I thought I should do: focus on work and finishing college. I bounced around from job to job trying to find where I fit in the world while still having the dream of becoming a published writer.

I focused so much on work, getting my college degree, writing fantasy fiction, and screenplays that my childhood feelings of inadequacy were shoved deep down into the back of my mind. I was successfully able to ignore those thoughts.

When I was working or doing my favorite solitary activity of writing, I consistently avoided speaking about my writing work in hopes that people would just eventually read my work and somehow, I would miraculously not have to speak about it. Thanks to Janet's book, *The Nature of Transformation* I now have the tools needed to heal from these past childhood events that had such a detrimental impact on my confidence therefore creating the inability to communicate and share my creative gifts with the world.

Janet Zavala's bravery and allowing herself to be vulnerable in this book by sharing her own stories of childhood trauma is admirable, and I felt a profound awakening in my soul and a newfound understanding of my own psyche when she says, "The effects of our experiences, although we believe we've put them in the past, will keep visiting us." Janet Zavala's words of wisdom made me realize that although I thought I had overcome my past childhood experiences of being ignored and bullied by peers and teachers, and the yearning to be liked, I really had not. The negative feelings these experiences created were still popping up like weeds. I realized this after reading: "The attributes of weeds mirror the attributes of our lingering fears in the form of our limiting beliefs. The longevity of a weed seed is long, as are the fears that were planted in our childhood. Weeds are adaptive." After reading this I realized that the moment I would think about being interviewed by a podcaster or journalist, necessary actions for marketing and pitching my book to film producers (my ultimate dream), are when my fears would sprout in my mind. Sadly, these fears had been getting in the way of being successful at something I so deeply loved. The most profound lesson I took away from this book is that once we clear the weeds from our minds as Janet Zavala states in *The Nature of Transformation*, we are able to grow, thrive, and transform back into the person we were meant to be before life's traumas cultivated our fears and doubts within.

The Nature of Transformation gives you the tools needed to become true to who you are, find the joy within your soul, heal with the inspiration of nature, and transform back into the person you were meant to be.

Gina Vallance

Author of *Amberly and the Secret of the Fairy Warriors*

Introduction

There's a tipping point in a person's life when the whispers of dreams placed on the shelf for far too long can no longer be ignored. There's an urgent need to stop letting the effects of past trauma steer life in directions never intended to travel. The nagging feeling that there must be more to life (more to achieve, more meaning, more contentment) hinders our happiness.

Individual and society's collective trauma has increased. Political and social unrest has been polarizing. Technological solutions that have been created for every potential human problem cannot fix the aching in our souls. In fact, these technology solutions take us further away from the healing properties of nature. Inadequate solutions and quick fixes abound; however, there are effective and powerful practices such as reconnecting to nature and meditation combined with coaching tools that allow you to understand yourself on a deeper soul level and create the life solutions that are designed by you for you.

The Nature of Transformation takes a comprehensive look at healing one's life — mind, body, and spirit. It offers a unique combination of traditional coaching principles (such as gaining clarity over a situation, developing goals, and a plan to achieve those goals) paired with powerful meditations, allowing the reader to focus their attention on the lessons they've learned, and the new awareness created. These healing modalities are presented with the backdrop of nature's transformative messages and gifts. The combination of these powerful techniques, along with my personal stories of healing and transformation, offers a distinctive approach to personal development.

Transformation isn't about changing who you are. It's getting back to the core of who you are and who you were meant to be before life's experiences created fear and doubt within you. This book provides a comprehensive look at all aspects of life, identifying where you might be losing energy and providing tactical steps to heal and transform your life and return to your *true nature*.

This book draws inspiration from nature and the seasons to show how transformation is necessary to grow, evolve and ultimately live a full and satisfying life. The attributes of the four seasons align with the transformational journey the reader is guided through. Spring represents new beginnings, rebirth, and rejuvenation. The information and exercises provided in this section direct the reader toward self-reflection and support them in purging stale beliefs that no longer serve them while planting seeds of new empowering beliefs. Summer's gift is an abundance of rich colors and beauty. The reader will learn how to nurture and sustain themselves by learning powerful thinking skills and increasing awareness. Fall is a time to gather, savor the wisdom achieved and celebrate the fruits of their labor while evolving and maturing. Here the reader will pay tribute to, and connect with, their spirit through the practices of forgiveness, gratitude, passionate living, and more. Winter brings muted colors and a barrenness that lends itself to focus on the essentials. Relying on resources gathered in the previous seasons, we begin to plan and prioritize the actions that will bring the most growth in the New Year.

I have been a seeker and an observer of my own healing throughout my life. My mother kidnapped me at nine years old, and I was exposed to and affected by other people's trauma responses for much of my life. For decades I read everything I could get my hands on, testing and practicing healing techniques but often remained lost and adrift. In *The Nature of Transformation,* I use my own experiences and the challenges I experienced during a traumatic childhood, a painful divorce, and my own healing as a model to show readers how they, too, can explore their own transformational healing.

There is no single formula for healing that works for everyone. There is no destination where happiness and contentment reside. We look for quick fixes, one book or one technique, that miraculously heals our life. Through my own healing and coaching others do the same, I've learned we need to pull and combine approaches and techniques to create the formula that works perfectly for us as individuals.

Each section will contain personal stories and my relationship, struggle, and healing within the topic area. I share important considerations and recommendations that the reader should consider in order to heal and gain alignment in this area of their life. I offer "Time with the Coach" and journal prompts, which include exploratory questions for readers to gain a deeper understanding of themselves and what is keeping them stuck in that area and co-create, with my assistance, solutions that are viable for them. Finally, at the end of each section, guided meditations are provided to ground the reader in what they've read and learned. The meditations come with essential oil recommendations, breathwork exercises, and empowering mantras

Healing and living our best lives are our individual responsibility. There is power and fear in this knowledge. I want to share with the world how to heal their lives and return to a place where they are living healthfully, on purpose, and with intention.

Healing and joyful living are daily practices. Consistent and intentional action over time enables the healing process to occur. This is what I offer the reader—the action steps needed to facilitate their own transformation—mind, body, and spirit.

SECTION One

Preparing For The Journey Ahead

Preparing for the Journey Ahead

EACH SECTION OF THIS book should be used and considered as a journey to greater self-awareness, understanding, and compassion. I provide you with my thoughts, ideas, stories, and the tools I use to navigate my own healing and transformation. I show you my vulnerability because I want you to be open to yours, owning your stories and your truth. Only through true vulnerability are you able to heal and overcome past wounds and experiences to start living the life you were meant to live.

> "Vulnerability sounds like truth and feels like courage. Truth and courage aren't always comfortable, but they're never weakness."
> —Brené Brown

I can't promise the process will be easy, but I do promise that if you persevere, it will be transformative. Where many programs leave off, this program gives you tangible actions and activities that you can use for a lifetime. The combined benefits of mantra, breath, meditation, journaling, gaining clarity through questioning, and action planning are significant. This powerful combination will allow you to accept deep into your cells that you were meant for greater things and will leave you with the belief that you can achieve them. It gives you a path to take to stop "playing small" in your life.

Grounding these practices in your mind, body, and spirit (a comprehensive approach to wellness) will allow you to infuse the teachings into your soul. Each element plays a critical role in your ability to fully accept your true nature. It gives you an anchor to come back to over and over whenever needed.

Nature is endlessly inspiring and fascinating. There are many similarities between nature's transformation and human transformation. Transformation is natural. It's a requirement. Nature, when presented with a crisis, responds to preserve itself in the most effective ways possible. It exists to show us its grandeur and expansiveness. Nature can be relentless but resets to often a more glorious version of itself. Allow yourself to deeply contemplate each section and your connection to nature's healing qualities.

The tools you'll find throughout the book:

Time with The Coach

As a practicing life coach and one who has received expert coaching, I understand the incredible benefits one on one time with a coach can bring. I will be your personal life coach throughout this journey. We will get to the heart of the barriers that exist for you as I help you gain clarity. Together, we'll explore areas where increased focus and awareness are needed. We will get to the root of your healing by exploring your experiences and the wounds you still carry. I will be challenging you and asking tough questions. Additional exercises will be provided to deepen the work, busting through the barriers still in front of you. Then finally, the coaching system takes you through action planning and establishing an accountability system.

Mantras

Mantras can pierce deeply into your subconscious and unconscious mind. They adjust and refocus your existing thoughts to those that are better for consumption than the replay of your negative and self-doubting thoughts. As you progress through each section in the coming days, weeks, or months, you will have a special mantra that will allow you to continue to come back to your true nature. Use these mantras in meditation or say them throughout the day. Mantras cut through the mental clutter and bring you back to a single truth.

Breathwork

Focused, healing breath allows you to release the tension you hold. It helps regulate emotions and brings your heart rate into a range that is optimal for your mental and physical performance. Breathing sustains life. Breathing intentionally and with the techniques provided enhances and recharges the energy your mind, body, and spirit need to thrive

Meditation

Meditation has changed my life, and I hope you find it life changing as well. Your meditation practice will evolve over time as you evolve. Meditation is a non-judgment activity. If you are doing it, you are doing it right. A sustained practice over time brings results. One session one time per week will not bring you the results you desire. So, please make meditation a priority in your life. Use the meditations to keep you centered, grounded, and focused on your own healing and your own journey. Use these meditations, especially in the morning, within 30 minutes of waking up and then throughout your day, as your schedule permits. These meditations are not long, only about five minutes. The guided meditations are not intended to be memorized. Read through the meditations provided and take in the essence and intent of the meditation into your own practice.

Journaling

Journaling is therapeutic, bringing everything you are discovering about yourself together. Take the opportunity to gather your thoughts and your learnings to reinforce each lesson. Journal when prompted but also journal whenever you feel the desire. As with any personal-development book, some ideas and concepts will impact you more than others. You will have the space and time to identify what was most important to you in each section, identify what resonated most, and what you learned about yourself. I'll also ask that you create a watch-list of areas where you know you struggle most. These are the sections of the book you'll want to make sure you return to as often as needed to get clarity and healing.

The case for journaling: When you write things down, you are engaging and stimulating different parts of your brain. Your brain will make stronger connections with the thoughts and feelings when you take the time to write them down. Relying on just thinking about these important concepts, you can easily become distracted—by choice, as an avoidance technique, or by life in general. When you commit your thoughts and experiences to writing, the information is more engrained in your mind and, therefore, works to reprogram your mind for positivity. It allows you to retain the good feelings you have about yourself. It will remind you of what you value about yourself and helps regulate negative emotions.

Settle in and get your pen ready. You will have plenty of opportunities to reflect on your experiences and thought processes. Grab a nice new journal, one that feels special because you'll be doing significant work in it.

Nature's Inspiration

Nature gives us countless gifts. She grounds us in our own true nature. She symbolizes resilience. I use the seasons as a metaphor for the healing journey and provide many opportunities for you to explore your own relationship with nature. I hope you're able to find inspiration from nature, just as I have.

One of the many ways Mother Nature heals our body, mind, and spirit is through the availability of herbs. They have a long history, dating back to ancient times, of providing health and medicinal benefits. Full of anti-inflammatory and antioxidant compounds, their healing properties are numerous.

Whether you grow your own, buy them from a farmers' market, or find them in other forms such as essential oils, they can be consumed as a boost of flavor in your food or enjoyed for their aromas in meditation and around your home.

Four of my favorites are sage, rosemary, lavender, and thyme. Use these herbs year-round based on the planting and harvesting conditions in your local area. When you use them, focus your attention on the herb's deeper spiritual symbolism. If you're using an herb during its indicated season, align with the seasonal transformation journey you are guided through in this book. Reflect and meditate on the healing gifts being offered.

Sage in Spring.

Sage's energy brings healing and blessings to you and the space that you use it in. Aligning with the messages we are given in spring, allow the sage to assist you in cleansing and washing away all that no longer serves you. Let the healing herb aid in the process of dissolving the limiting thoughts and beliefs you have about yourself and life. Sage signifies the purification of spiritual and physical energies, so turn to it to begin your healing journey.

Rosemary in Summer.

Rosemary is associated with Aphrodite, the goddess of love and beauty. As summer arrives with an abundance of colors and beauty, invoke the gifts of rosemary to create greater awareness of the love you have for yourself. Demonstrate that love by feeding your mind with nourishing and empowering information while learning ways in which you can deepen self-love.

Lavender in Fall.

Fall is a time for reconnecting to our spirit. Lavender symbolizes connection and enlightenment. It has a calming effect and brings with it peace of mind. Use the healing properties of lavender to explore deeper connections with yourself and others, practice gratitude, and identify ways to release anger and resentment.

Thyme in Winter.

Thyme symbolizes letting the past go and moving forward with strength and courage; in fact, in Ancient Greece, soldiers placed thyme in their bathwater for that very purpose. As you bring another year to a close and begin to plan the next year, use thyme to inspire you to make bold choices and attract prosperity.

1.1 I Honor Your Journey

Early in my 20s, I told someone who experienced extreme trauma in their life to "just get over it." I regret my insensitivity and immaturity. My experiences had not yet given me a full view of the world. Far too many people in the field of self-development preach positivity as if it is merely a light switch that can be turned on and off. Just think positive thoughts! Ready? Go!

Our lives and our brains don't work like that. The approach used in *The Nature of Transformation* honors all that you've been through. It respects the fact that you may be suffering from the effects of trauma, depression, anxiety, chronic pain, or other afflictions. This method also respects that you need to break down barriers and be given a push to make progress on your goals. It is not meant to replace medical or therapeutic support. But, as you know, the work continues after the visit to the doctor's office.

The work that we'll do here is an exploration into the most impactful events of your life and how they continue to influence the way you feel about yourself and the choices you make. We will explore what there is to learn from the experiences. Some things that happen are senseless; even so, these events have formed the person you are today. They may have saddled you with fears, but they have also given you incredible strengths. We'll honor these lessons together and see how we can turn these tools you've developed into usable assets. Where possible, you will learn to let go of the beliefs that no longer serve you.

The effects of our experiences, although we believe we've put them in the past, keep visiting us. An assault, molestation or sexual abuse, the loss of a child, and countless other things stick with us because these events have pierced our souls. I can't, and I won't be so callous to say, "get over it," or "just think positive thoughts." I will provide you with the tools to navigate those times when memories or triggers are impacting you most.

Life continues, and we are constantly presented with events that bring us sadness or anger. The coping skills developed here will be with you for a lifetime, to return to whenever needed. This is the safe space that honors your true nature.

1.2 Transformation

> "You and I possess within ourselves – at every moment of our lives, under all circumstances, the power to transform the quality of our lives. Knowing that is what the work is all about."
> —Werner Erhard

You are on a journey to (re)becoming more of who you truly are. You already have the skills and abilities to be the best you. At your core, you are loved with unlimited potential and a pure heart. Life events and the people around you have influenced you to become timid or scared. These circumstances made you believe lies about yourself—that you are unworthy, unable to achieve success, or live the life of your dreams. This is what you will change. By doing the work, you will be able to remove the negative thought patterns and transform yourself back into the truth of who you truly are.

Can people change? Everyone experiences hundreds, maybe thousands, of catalysts for change throughout their lifetimes. So, the real question becomes: How can people avoid changing? Change is in our nature. It is in the biology of our cells. You have already changed so much in your lifetime and will continue to change. Your physical body is in a constant state of change from the moment you are born. Also in a state of constant evolution are your opinions, your surroundings, the people you associate with, and your profession. You have changed your thoughts and the way you perceive people and events. With each phase of your life, you have experienced a tremendous amount of change.

The act of simply living requires transformation. All life forms are non-exempt—it is our true nature. When movement stops, life stops. Pain is a result of trying to halt this evolution. Many people suffer in the resistance. Transformation is our natural state. There is no reason you cannot find your way back to your true self now and experience the miraculous transformation for which you have been longing.

During a transformative time in my life, I was feeling stuck in a life that was patched together by my pain, fears, and unfulfilled ambitions. I knew, somehow, I had created this reality but that it was built on a faulty foundation of conscious and unconscious bad choices and disempowering thoughts. I wasn't entirely sure how I got there or what I needed to do to get out. I was feeling hopelessly stuck, unable to make a move without hurting myself or hurting someone else. There's a sharp pain in your gut, an ache, a knowing when you know it's time to make a big change. You can either ignore that ache until it returns (because it will return), or you can take the opportunity to answer the calling your intuition has been signaling to you.

I embarked on my journey of healing. Seeking my own transformation, tending my garden. It has been a journey to learn who I am, learn more about others, and find my passion and joy. I learned to embrace the not-so-pretty truths about myself, healing the wounds of my past along the way. I learned to forgive myself and forgive others while forging a new life for myself.

I studied—formally and by myself. I took bits and pieces of everything I learned and created my own formula for success. I did the work, and I am still doing the work. We are all a work in progress—to the end. I found my light and realized where my power was all along. I designed a life I now lead purposefully and with intention.

We all have our stories, our experiences, and our journeys—our landscape. Even the really bad stuff makes us the people we are. Especially the bad stuff.

1.3 New Beginnings

> "No river can return to its source, yet all rivers must have a beginning." —Indigenous Proverb

It is my strong belief that we, as humans, crave new beginnings. It is our way of evolving and growing. It is an innate calling in all of us. Our soul requires growth. The deep spiritual side within us all requires us to expand our experiences by learning more about ourselves and the world around us. Transformation and new beginnings are about testing the limits of our greatest potential.

Change can be difficult. We resist change because it's scary not knowing what's on the other side of our transformation. We get accustomed to feeling and living a certain way. Impending changes often tap into the place where our deepest insecurities lie. Doubts about our worthiness and ability to change emerge. We worry about our continued lovability if we make a change that may, in turn, transform us and make us whole, afraid of the reaction of those closest to us. Transformation isn't about abandoning your life, all that you've built, or loved ones. It's about integration and adaptation.

Knowing that transformation is an inevitability, the best tactic is to approach it with intentionality instead of leaving it in the hands of chance. Welcome it in versus fighting its inescapable arrival. Not all change is unexpected. We often can see the tides of change on the horizon. Paying attention and having an awareness of what you're seeing and feeling will give you insight. This will enable you to not only prepare but also to plan how you will thrive during and after the change occurs. Change tends to show up in three distinct ways: 1) as a soul cry to adjust your course to return to your true nature, 2) change that naturally occurs in the seasons of our lives; from children to empty nesting; from new jobs, losing jobs, to retirement, and 3) unexpected changes arising from tragedy or trauma that catapults us into rapid change with no warning like a sudden death of a loved one, being let go from your employment with no warning, or countless other ways in which change arises unexpectedly.

A soul cry can often be felt in your gut. Your intuition is telling you that it's time to make a change. It might feel like boredom, discontent, or even anger that your current circumstances are not going as expected. Perhaps it's not achieving what you want to achieve with your health, relationships, spirituality, finances, or in other areas of your life. I find that there's often a tipping point in someone's life when they realize that after doing all the things there were *supposed* to do, there remains an aching and a longing for what it is they *want* to do. And sometimes, it transcends wanting. That ache then becomes a dire need. They feel almost commanded to accomplish that dream or reach the goal that they have put on the back burner of their life for so long. They may even know what that "thing" is but may be carrying around a long list of why they can't or won't be able to achieve it.

There are changes, welcome or not, that can be easily predicted. If you have children, they will likely one day leave your home and build their own lives. This can be jarring for some people who have dedicated a lot of their time and energy towards raising their kids while neglecting their own wants and desires. When that level of energy is no longer needed, and the inevitability of the new reality has not been planned for, this can leave parents bereft. Unfortunately, the divorce rate for first marriages is 41% in the United States and is even higher for second and third marriages. Many people struggle to make the decision to end their marriage or stay together. Whether a marriage ends or not, change as a result of saving a marriage or ending a marriage is not something that spontaneously occurs. Career planning and planning for your life after your career should be approached with intention and attention.

There is the type of change that is forced upon us through no design of our own. Perhaps it's an unexpected job loss, a death, or some other major life event that could not be predicted. You have no choice but to answer the call and pick yourself up to meet the challenges presented. You make the necessary adjustment in your life to survive. Oftentimes, the change presented offers a growth opportunity. You learned something new about yourself and gained more confidence, knowing you can not only survive but thrive.

Somehow, even knowing the inevitability of change, we resist new beginnings. We feel we must choose correctly. We often feel like we must make the right choice, especially if we're torn between two paths. Jake Abel said wisely, "The only wrong choice is not making one." The truth is, there is no right choice, and there is no wrong choice. Assigning virtue to one path over another is a recipe for inertia and will further delay the necessary action you must take. You may feel more drawn towards one decision over another. You must know that each choice, each decision, and every step you take is the exact right action you need to take at that moment. It will lead you to the next thing, and the next thing and so on. So, don't worry if it's the right choice; worry if you're unable to choose at all.

> "There are two mistakes one can make along the road to truth… not going all the way, and not starting."—Buddha

Every year, I make a New Year's wish (not a resolution, but a wish) that I have a scary year. Because having a scary year, in this context, means that I am doing new things, busting through my comfort zone, and taking chances with the intention. I embrace the fear because I know the source and the remedy of my own fears. The fears don't disappear. They simply stop dictating my responses. When you're able to choose and design your own path, no matter how outlandish, the experience and results will be exponentially more satisfying than if the easy, unchanged road was taken.

The fears that we have are real. At least the existence of them is. They were created from our experiences—both past and present. When has the command to "just stop being afraid" ever worked to eliminate fear? It hasn't. Although the fear that you feel is real, it is likely untrue. When past trauma embeds fear into our minds and body, the outcome is often catastrophized. Therefore, we must identify the source of the fear and take intentional action to begin to turn down the volume of the fear-based voices and turn up the volume of the encouraging thoughts and beliefs. Common fears around change and new beginnings and suggestions to counteract them include:

Feeling we won't be accepted or supported along our journey. There are people in our lives who may be impacted by our decisions. It is simply the way we humans exist. Sometimes we make up scenarios in our heads about the reactions others will have when we are making a choice and making a change. Oftentimes, these negative outcome scenarios are our own fears manifesting to stop us from acting. Have a conversation with those closest to you and most affected by the choices you make. Strategize, negotiate, and support one another in your life's journey. Don't set up a tent along the pathway of life and never progress forward.

Our choices are (truly) not supported by others. The statement, "Their reaction has more to do with them than it does you," couldn't be truer. If someone is not supporting you, it is *their* fear projected onto you. What are they afraid of? Are they afraid of losing you? Are they afraid you will reject or outgrow them as you embark on your own growth journey? Are they afraid to face their own challenges head-on? Have a conversation about the source of their fears? If you're unable to support those around you on their journey and they are unable to support you, perhaps there is a co-dependency that is preventing you both from reaching your full potential.

Fear of failure. Especially if we're starting this journey a little later in life, we feel there isn't enough time to test and fail. We want to get it right. Additionally, we worry about what it will say about us if we fail. What will people think? Do you want to know what they are likely to think? They will think, "Damn, wasn't she brave to try. I wish I was that courageous. Look at all she's learned and watch her pivot. Look at where she's going now. She is an inspiration." You will inspire someone else's bravery. Don't rob the world of watching you go for your dreams.

Fear of success. Maybe even more frightening than the fear of failure is the fear of success. How will our comfortably uncomfortable lives change if we succeed in what we want? How will this affect those around us or our life circumstances? Often women will play it safe and play it small not to upset the environment around them. Marianne Williamson wrote, in part in her book, A *Return to Love,* "Our deepest fear is not that we are inadequate. Our deepest fear is that we are powerful beyond measure." We are often afraid of our own power. It's time for all of us to stop playing small and claim the full power we are capable of possessing.

> "I realize there's something incredibly honest about trees in winter, how they're experts at letting things go." —Jeffrey McDaniel

Transformation is not an all-or-nothing proposition. Leaving your job, your family, or your home is not required to begin a transformational journey. When we fear change, we tend to think in absolutes. The all-or-nothing mindset is what trips us up and has us resisting the change that is inevitable.

Transformation is truly about the journey. I know you've heard this adage a million times. The fact is it couldn't be truer. Transformation is not about the *thing* we acquire or achieve. If done with an awareness of self, the purpose is what we learn about ourselves and the pursuit of reaching our highest potential. It's about overcoming those internal blocks that prevent us from taking a chance and making a change.

You don't need to give up what you currently have to create a new beginning. New beginnings are not about restriction and limitation. It is about expansion. Expanding those areas in your life that you secretly (and maybe openly) dream about. The *either/or* mindset needs to go away. This is a *both/and* world. You can achieve your dreams *and* take loving care of your family.

Your comfort zone really isn't that comfortable. Why would you want to get out of your comfort zone? It's—well—comfortable! Maybe not so much. What it is—is familiar. Evolutionarily, we were predisposed to remain with people in situations and maintain certain behaviors because of the perception that it would keep us safe from harm. We no longer live in those conditions; therefore, the perception and reality of safety have shifted.

Furthermore, comfort is rarely satisfying for too long. We settle in, get comfortable, then we need to change positions. This is the cyclical nature of life and the transformation we *must* experience.

If you try something new or put yourself out there, I can absolutely promise you that you will feel a certain level of fear and doubt. It comes with the territory. If you're not feeling fear, I will maintain that maybe you're not taking a big enough chance.

On the other hand, familiarity and comfort can be nice. As a result of maintaining this nice feeling, however, you'll likely have an incessant and stubborn nagging of what could have been if you, indeed, took the chance.

What we desire doesn't auto-magically show up. We need to usher it in. For many years, I wished and attempted to invoke *The Secret* to usher in the life I was meant to live. My first problem with that approach is that I wasn't clear on what it was I really wanted. I could give you a list of things I didn't want, but I had not explored my desires enough to know what it was that I did want.

The second problem with that approach is that typically situations and people don't just show up on our doorstep, announcing "Change has arrived!" We first need to get clear on what we want and really infuse these desires into our DNA. Once we do that, the steps we need to take to make that dream a reality will materialize and become clearer. You first must see it, feel it, then you can experience it.

Consistent action over time will bring the change you desire.

The first step is admitting to yourself that you want something new in your life.

Sometimes new beginnings are forced on us and are not what we would have chosen, and yet, they are presented to us as an opportunity to grow and evolve. At times, the fear can be overwhelming. Use the tips below to bust through the fear you feel when you are feeling resistance to a life transformation.

1. Search for the lesson. If you're experiencing a change that is not of your choosing, ask yourself, "What opportunities are available here for me?" and "What is there to learn about myself or the universe?"

2. Let go of expectations of perfection. When you're starting something new, having really high expectations of a perfect outcome can be dangerous. It's dangerous because when it is not perfect (perfection is a myth anyway), you may become demotivated to continue. As Voltaire is credited with saying, "Perfect is the enemy of good."

3. Stop future tripping. Identifying every worst-case scenario is your fear manifesting itself. "What-if-ing" yourself to death before you even begin will ensure that you will never arrive at your destination. Check and debunk your assumptions. Challenge your what-ifs.

4. Accept what is. "Well, if I had this or that, I'd be able to achieve my goals." Lamenting about the perfect circum-

stances to begin your transformative journey is counterproductive. Accept the conditions that exist right now and work from there.

5. Embrace change as a natural part of life. We can't fight it. It will happen. Keep in mind that the universe is tricky. If you try too hard to hold onto things just as they are, she'll likely come along and force you into some sort of change. Preempt her by embracing change.

6. Recognize the foundational good things that exist in your life right now. You have everything you need to begin your journey. You don't have to wait for a season, a situation, or a better time. If you need more knowledge in a certain area, there are tons of free resources available. If you need more in-depth learning, there are paid options. The time you delay getting started, you can never get back.

7. Regroup, reassess, and re-inventory. Taking a step back to assess your current situation and evaluating where you need to go is not delaying progress. It's actually assisting in the organization process so that you can move forward with ease. Take inventory of the knowledge, skills, and abilities you possess. It's okay to regroup before moving forward. This counts as a step in the right direction.

8. Get back up. Things rarely go as planned. We may be disappointed or even rejected. That's ok. It really is. Don't stop. Keep pushing. The universe put this obstacle in your way to test your resolve and commitment. If you need to take time to reassess, do it. Every step and misstep are

exactly what you need to get to the next level. Get back up with a newfound fierceness.

9. Think big but act small. I want you to dream BIG. But when it comes to acting, understand that small actions done consistently get you to the finish line. The problem is that we live in a society and maintain a mindset of instant gratification and progress. We want to see those big gains and huge wins. We get frustrated when we don't see immediate results.

YOUR TRANSFORMATION MEDITATION

ESSENTIAL OILS

Place a drop or two of the essential oil in the palm of your hand. Rub your hands together, then gently inhale the fragrance. Take a few deep breaths as you find a comfortable position for the meditation below.

Peppermint essential oil signifies change and will help stimulate the memory of who you are at your core. Sweetgrass and sweet orange essential oils also signify transformation.

YOUR TRANSFORMATION MANTRA

I have the power to transform my life.
I AM *transforming my life.*

TRANSFORMATION BREATH

Inhale for six seconds, expanding the belly and filling the bottom of the lungs.

Exhale slowly for six seconds, emptying the belly completely.

Repeat 15 times for maximum effect.

YOUR TRANSFORMATION MEDITATION

Sit in a comfortable position, spine straight.

Do the breathing sequence above to begin.

Continue normal, relaxed breathing.

In your mind's eye, see a caterpillar's cocoon. Imagine a beautiful butterfly forming in the cocoon. The butterfly is working hard to become its expansive, new, free self.

Imagine your own transformation. Visualize what you will look like and how you will feel when you have transformed into your true nature.

Imagine your confidence.

Imagine the self-assurance you have.

Imagine living the life of your own creation.

Imagine having the feeling of certainty and gratitude.

Imagine yourself as clear-headed and effective.

Sit with those feelings for just a moment.

When you're ready, slowly open your eyes.

Carry these feelings with you throughout your day.

As you come back to room awareness, slowly open your eyes. Give yourself a moment.

Take the time to write any notes about the thoughts or feelings that may have come up during your meditation.

1.4 Your Nature

"Look deep into nature, and then you will understand everything better."—Albert Einstein

You are an extension of source energy. Source energy is the part of every human that is non-physical. It is our soul, our intuition, our goodness, and our life-giving force. It is called many things throughout the world: chi, prana, ki, mana. It is the part of us that existed before we came into our bodies. It is the part of us that will exist after we exit our human form. The source energy within us is also our connection to the Divine, universal power, or simply the power greater than us, whatever belief system you honor.

Source energy is perfect, kind, loving, and nurturing—and by extension—so are you. This is your natural programming, your true nature. It is space we are all seeking to return to—before life's circumstances modified our original programming. Your life experiences created the perception you have of yourself. These events distorted your thoughts and made you believe you were something less than perfect. They made you believe that somehow you were unworthy or unable to have the fulfillment and happiness you deserve.

Perfection needs to be redefined and rebranded. Perfection exists when its source is from within. You were born perfect. You were born with exactly the right number of skills, abilities, and attributes. Your soul, spirit, or energy, at its core, is perfect. Your perfection is unalterable. External perfection is trying to meet someone else's standards. External perfection, perfect behavior or doing a perfect job is a fallacy. It's a mask. Striving for external perfection keeps you stuck and keeps you from realizing your true inner perfection.

Life's journey and life's purpose are to get back to the state of remembering and believing this to be true. Your purpose is to return to the state of accepting and loving yourself just as you are. The most interesting people I know are complex, with their uniqueness on display for all to see. These people have lived life and survived challenging events in their lives, and still, their light shines bright.

YOUR NATURE MEDITATION

ESSENTIAL OILS

Place a drop or two in the palm of your hand. Rub your hands together, then gently inhale the fragrance. Take a few deep breaths as you find a comfortable position for the meditation below.

Use eucalyptus, rosemary, or cedarwood essential oils for their earthiness and to deepen this meditation. Eucalyptus energizes and revitalizes. Rosemary has a calming effect, allowing our body to release the stress hormone cortisol. Cedarwood has anti-inflammatory properties.

YOUR NATURE MANTRA

I am perfect, kind, and loving, just as I am.

YOUR NATURE BREATHING TECHNIQUE

Take a deep breath to the count of five and release it completely, counting to five.

Repeat this breath five more times.

Return to normal, relaxed breathing.

YOUR NATURE MEDITATION

Go out into nature. Find someplace, whether it be in your backyard, your local park, or a state park. You may be by the ocean or a lake, out in the desert, in the mountains, in a forest, or in the middle of a cornfield. Find a comfortable and safe place to sit. If you can, take off your shoes and feel the earth beneath your feet or under your legs. Gently close your eyes, relax, and drop your shoulders. Place your hands on your thighs, palms up, resting comfortably.

Now, just listen. Continue breathing. Notice the sounds of nature. Block out other sounds like cars, barking dogs, lawnmowers, or any other industrial sounds. Do you hear birds singing? Notice the different songs they are singing. Is there a breeze? Can you hear the wind rustle the trees? Do you hear the sounds of water?

Now feel the ground even more solid against your body. Can you feel a breeze on your skin, on your face, in your hair?

What can you smell? Are there fragrant plants and flowers?

Sit comfortably with the symphony of nature and all its sounds, smells, and touches.

Take your time here. You don't have anywhere you need to be.

When you're ready, slowly bring yourself into awareness.

As you complete your meditation, understand that you are one with nature. There is nothing that separates you from nature or from your own nature.

As you come back to room awareness, slowly open your eyes. Give yourself a moment.

Take the time to write any notes about the thoughts or feelings that may have come up during your meditation.

1.5 Your Purpose

Your purpose is not your vocation. When searching for your purpose in a career, you feel dissatisfied and unfulfilled.

I have worked for large companies that employ thousands of people. I have never heard anyone express that their job at these companies is their life's purpose. Many of these people, however, can find satisfaction in the work they do. They are often very skilled and effective. They can achieve the level of success they desire, surrounded by smart, challenging, and good people. Many may feel passion for what they do—a talent for negotiation, the rush of a sale, the accomplishment of a successful project, or the thoughtfulness of providing excellent service to others. A lucky few get to combine their passions with their vocation, but your life's purpose is not defined by a job.

Your life's purpose is YOU.

Modern pop psychology has trended for decades to implore us to find our purpose. The implication is to find this purpose outside of ourselves. Our purpose is not outside of ourselves. Our purpose *is* us. We are put on this earth to be whole and happy, and through achieving wholeness, we can do the things that we are passionate about and bring our fully realized gifts to the world. The external search for purpose causes anxiety and leaves us unfulfilled. When we tap into our own true nature and work towards creating happiness and joy in our lives, the activities that we're supposed to do will naturally materialize. Our purpose here on earth is *not* that activity. Our purpose is to create, maintain, and prepare our mind, body, and spirit to receive the lessons and progress into a more evolved soul.

My definition of success has evolved over time. When I was growing up in a small town in Illinois, success to me was defined more by what I did not want. Choices seemed limited. And I did not like the choices laid out in front of me. When I moved to California at the age of 19 and entered the workforce, success was being able to do a good job, being recognized, promoted, and given additional responsibilities. This definition was destroyed, mostly by my inability to set healthy boundaries, so I ended up being overworked and stressed. When I landed back on my feet at another large corporation, I saw success through academics by getting my college degree and continuing to advance in title and responsibility (now with healthier boundaries). Ultimately, I was able to learn by working with my employees what I was good at and really enjoyed doing.

Today I define my personal success as being able to effectively serve others through the coaching process and my writing. However, my life's purpose is still trying to make myself a complete, happy, and whole person. When I am feeling healthy and whole, I'm able to help more people effectively. I am also able to enjoy any success that may come to me because I'm not overwhelmed with negative thinking that I'm not worthy of the success I have achieved.

You were meant to show up fully and whole in this world, bringing to the world joy, love, and caring. And, oh boy, don't we need a lot of that?

Breathe a sigh of relief and take this truth into your heart and soul. You are perfect the way you are. There are fundamental things about you that are your unique gifts. The other stuff—the hang-ups and the fears and the negative thought patterns—those are not you. Those things have been manufactured as a response to conditions over time. Those are the things that we will start to wash away through this process to get you back to your natural state.

The Nature of Transformation is a tool to manifest your life's purpose of bringing a full and complete *you* to this world.

1.6 Your Landscape

> "There are no lines in nature, only areas of color, one against another."—Edouard Manet

The strength and wisdom you possess now are a direct result of your past experiences. Celebrate and be grateful for this wisdom. Your stories and unique qualities create a diverse picture of who you are. Like a field of wildflowers, each color, shape, and petal are uniquely you. You are beautiful and vibrant. Honor your stories. Honor your colors.

There was a point in time when I realized that the way I had been living was no longer bearable and the discomfort of staying stuck exceeded the discomfort of making a change. I tried to reason my way through it. I tried to convince myself that it would be okay. I thought, "I'll just stay here; it won't be too bad if I don't move around much. I'll make as little noise as possible and do what I need to do to survive each day. I'll just go along with the program." But I could not stay still. I squirmed uncontrollably (the body's natural reaction to confinement). I needed to change positions. Growing angry with myself, I thought, "Why can't I just be still?" This was followed by the sickening realization that I didn't need to move to feel pain. In fact, it hurt even worse to stay still. The pain and depression remained no matter what I did. There is an undeniable knowing when you need to act. The feeling, the desire, cannot be suppressed any longer.

This is my landscape, borne out of my choices and experiences. I begin my story with the moment I realized that I needed transformation. I believe that everyone experiences that moment when you realize that you must embark on a healing journey to begin your own personal transformation. After the journal break below, I continue to reveal how my experiences created strengths in me while also exposing the fears and doubts that kept me from making progress in my life for far too long. By sharing my landscape, my hope is that you open to your own and release any shame you may have carried with you.

Journal Break – Moment of Reflection

Are you grappling with a similar situation? Are you feeling compelled to make a shift? Are you feeling tired and worn down by the constant struggle to hold onto something that has exceeded its expiration date? What area (or areas) in your life do you *know* cannot continue as it has been? What areas of your life do you struggle with or fill you with doubt? Work or career? Relationships? Health? Family? Money? Your physical environment? List the areas in which you want to see change or improvement. List the areas where life overwhelms you. Briefly describe why these areas are unsatisfying and why it's important at this moment to make a change.

Soon after I decided to make one of my big moves, I was sitting on my couch, drowning in my pain and tears. I scribbled, "The exit from hell burns most at the exit. That's where the hottest heat and the raging fire are. Just get past the exit to hell, and you'll be fine." For my own survival, my marriage needed to end. I'd been stuck in a cycle of fear and codependency for twenty years. I was avoiding the painful next step. In my gut, I knew the wounds would heal if I could make it through the fiery walls. If I stayed in the hell of my own creation, never attempting to get out, I would be stuck, and the pain would be never-ending.

In writing that line, I was expressing not only the pain I was currently in but also a deep knowing that this was the price to pay for the healing I needed. I knew it was essential for me to push past the inferno and through the pain to get to the other side.

First, I needed big doses of truth. I started to heal my burns and slowly ease the pain. I had to walk through some deep wounds—some brand new, others buried by layers of denial.

It would have been easy to look only at my most recent turmoil and struggle, but I needed to understand how I got there. There was a reason I continued to allow chaos into my life while nearing my fortieth birthday. I needed to address the source of my pain.

I had to begin at the beginning. Childhood memories and verbal/nonverbal cues impact your beliefs about yourself long after you grow up. My childhood was chaotic and lonely, confusing, and frightening at times.

I began to separate from my true nature when my mom left my dad and her four children (me, my older brother and two older sisters) for another man. It was the mid-1970s, and the sickness of silence, whether it was the times or just my family home, was the norm. Nobody explained to seven-year-old me what was going on, not even on a basic level.

It was a confusing time. One moment I was looked after, with someone making sure I took baths and got to school, and the next, I wasn't. I learned that I needed to wash up after a kid at school mistook the dirt on my neck for a birthmark. I learned I needed to start walking to school about the time I saw the other kids in the neighborhood heading that way.

My mom reappeared a few weeks later to take me to an amusement park, which, even at my age, felt like a combination of a bait and switch and a bribe. I was the youngest and seemingly most pliable child to introduce to this new person in my mom's life. It would not be the last time I felt like I was "cheating" on my family, especially my dad, with a replacement life and a replacement father.

To finalize the divorce, a scary judge asked each of us kids who we wanted to live with. My two sisters chose my mom, and my brother chose my dad. I was unwilling to show favoritism for one parent over the other, so a choice was made for me. I was shipped off—away from my family home and the only school I had ever known, to a dingy apartment building and an unfamiliar new school ten minutes away.

That began a year or more of extreme chaos. My brothers and sisters moved back and forth between our dad's house and our mom's apartment. I was alone a lot. I witnessed physical violence, a lot of drinking, and an attempted suicide or two. Once I watched my mom being rolled out of the apartment on a stretcher after trying to overdose. Another time, my dad busted open the bathroom door to carry my sister to his car, then to the nearest hospital. Silence prevailed. Sad and broken people just returned and acted as if nothing had happened. I was merely the invisible, silent observer of the madness and chaos.

The broken doorknob in the bathroom in my dad's house would be a constant reminder of the fear and sadness over the next fifteen years. When my brother finally fixed it during one of his stays in the house on Los Padres Drive, it left another layer of sorrow. That broken doorknob was the only evidence of what had occurred that day. Once the door could be closed completely and locked, the event disappeared from reality, never to be spoken of in our already fractured family.

I still live ten minutes away from the apartment building that served as a stopping point as my family tried to flee their pain. I still pass it on my way to the freeway. For a long time, I lived in morbid curiosity, always trying to remember what I was feeling when I lived there and hoping to catch a glimpse of the lost and lonely girl sitting on the concrete stairs next to the pool. I still hope for a red light in front of the building so I can take a long look inside. Yet I'm grateful when the light is green, and I don't have to pause at those memories.

Ultimately, my siblings chose to remain in the more stable home my dad provided; I was left alone with my emotionally broken mom. She decided to escape back to her childhood home to seek solace with her emotionally abusive mother. With the help of my aunt, we stole away one pre-dawn morning and boarded a Greyhound bus headed for the Midwest. I was eight years old.

It was just Mom and me at that point, and, given the departure hour, there were no tearful goodbyes from family as we boarded the bus. No one, aside from my aunt, knew we had left. When we were positioned in our seats, I asked Mom where we were going. For the first time, she told me that we were moving from California to Illinois.

Technically, that's kidnapping.

The smell of diesel fuel still brings me back to that dark bus traveling from one sad bus stop to the next, pulling up at various times of the night to truck stops and restaurants filled with people living on the outskirts of a "normal" life. They were either permanently transient or temporarily transitioning to a new life and, I imagine, driven by pain or some personal crisis, as we were. I was so young, but I could relate to those people. No home, no roots, no grounding. The smell of diesel fuel continues to spark those feelings of fear and loneliness. It brings a sadness that I spent too many years trying to cover up.

I'm not even sure how long it was before I talked to the rest of my family, but it was likely six months or more. I assumed no one was looking for me or realized we were gone, which added an additional layer of trauma and a belief that my existence really didn't matter much to the people I was closest to. These events, like all the others, were never spoken of. The toxic silence continued.

Journal Break – Moment of Reflection

Do you have a similar story? We've all likely survived (or are still trying to survive) a significant trauma or event that left us with feelings of betrayal, guilt, anger, or fear. Reflect on any times in your life when you felt these life-altering emotions. Take out your journal. Write what comes up for you. Let the words flow onto the paper.

If it feels right to you, practice some radical self-care. Consider taking a break or a warm bath or going into nature to experience her restorative effects. Take the next action that feels right to you. We often have shared experiences, and if it feels safe, you may feel like talking to someone who was a witness to your past. My brother and I have compared notes about what happened, telling our own versions of shared events.

My mom and I arrived in central Illinois after a four-day bus ride. We were greeted at the bus stop by her younger brother and his three daughters. My middle cousin was in the fourth grade, as was I; my youngest cousin was a year younger than me, and the eldest was three years older. I cannot recall the sound of my uncle's voice, but I know he was a quiet, caring man. I remember him caring for his mother and adoring girls.

It was clear, however, from the moment we met at that bus stop that at least two of his daughters did not adore *me*. I had left Southern California, with its dense population and perfect perpetual summer and arrived in a frigid town with miles and miles of snow-covered flatlands. It was a shock to my system, made even worse by three curious girls wondering what I was doing invading their space.

My oldest cousin was around eleven years old and extremely close to our grandmother. They shared a special bond. My mom and I had just settled in at Grandma's one-bedroom house when my cousin, who lived six doors down the road, burst through the door in an absolute panic. She was crying, yelling, and repeating, "You're going to take my grandma away from me; you're going to steal my grandma!"

She then dove underneath the bed while I, despite my fear and confusion, tried to console her, saying, "I'm not going to take grandma away from you." I was scared in this new environment and felt a deep need for people to like and accept me. I needed allies, but she felt threatened by me. I shrank, even more, trying to be less threatening, trying to be more invisible. I became skilled at making myself small.

Things normalized as much as they could for my crazy situation. Mom and I moved to a single-wide trailer; I adjusted to my new school. I visited California one summer when I was eleven or so, only to return to Illinois and discover that Mom was married to a guy I'd never met. This new "daddy" sharing our cramped space drank—a lot—so my mom drank more too.

Around the same time, my brother, who had gotten himself into a fair amount of trouble in California, was shipped to Illinois to live with us. Since the trailer had only two bedrooms, I slept in the living room on a small twin bed. My stepfather would fall asleep (or pass out) in my "bedroom" while he was watching TV, snoring ferociously.

My brother used his California mystique, charm, and artistic talent to become annoyingly popular in our little farm-town high school. During the two years that we lived together in that single-wide, two-bedroom trailer, not a word passed between us. We were reenacting our mom's family's special form of dysfunction of not talking with each other for years, decades, or lifetimes. There was no intervention from my mother, which compounded my isolation.

All the while, I was turning into an awkward, introverted, lonely, and confused teenager. The feeling that stays with me is being relegated to a dark corner, like the one my bed was in. I felt pushed aside, disregarded, and ignored.

Journal Break – Moment of Reflection

Have you ever felt all alone, ignored, or isolated? Maybe you, too, experienced neglect as a child, or perhaps it was the opposite, with too much focus, attention, and expectation placed upon you. Whatever our childhood was like, we often, even when surrounded by a lot of people, have overwhelming feelings of being misunderstood or alone. Take a moment to reflect on a time you had these feelings. How and when do these feelings continue to show up for you today?

Take the opportunity to write out your stories, as I've done above. It is very cathartic to release these stories on paper, so they are no longer trapped solely in your memories and psyche.

Thankfully, my life was more stable during high school. A year after graduating, I packed up my car and set off to California, caravanning with a friend. I was finally going home. She went to her aunt's house in San Diego; I went to live with my older sister and her son.

The next twenty years were more weeds than flowers; however, there was at least one magnificent bloom.

Newly transplanted to Southern California, I got a job and then ran straight into a man who was even more damaged than me. I was nineteen, and he was twenty-two. He embodied more hurt than I could ever conceive in a person. He was someone who loved deeply and poetically but also had profound sadness, anger, and violence oozing from his pores.

For the most part, he tried to keep that shadow side from me, but when it is part of your composition, it affects every part of your life, as well as the lives of those close to you. This was certainly the case with us. His volatility and my insecurities combined to make a bitter cocktail as he took his anger and pain out on the world, and I desperately tried to make someone prove that they loved me. Our relationship reaffirmed my wounds and amplified my pain. It took the fear I already had and created new dimensions that I could not have conceived.

If I was afraid of abandonment before, I was paralyzed by it now. If I had battled loneliness and isolation before, now it enveloped me. If I felt unworthy of being loved before, now I was certain of that unworthiness. There was authentic beauty at times, but the strong current of our individual and collective pain threatened us daily.

Our beautiful son, born when I was twenty-three, was the magnificent flower I mentioned. The rest of these twenty years were spent floating in and out of denial. I was hopeful that somehow our dysfunctional relationship would become palatable, and when it didn't, I would be consumed with disappointment, self-loathing, and anger.

One of my inherited weeds is being a martyr. Before I realized I needed to end my marriage, I decided (a thoughtful, sane decision) that I would sacrifice my life and happiness to try to make my husband well. Maybe you've had the same thoughts. Maybe you've thought, "If I just sacrifice enough, it will eventually be okay." This thinking ends with the acceptance of an eternally unhappy and unfulfilled life or the undeniable feeling that a change is the only thing that will allow you to survive. In my case, the decision to forfeit a happy life to fix another was genuine and influenced by an awful book I'd read.

Far too many people fall into this same trap of living solely to make others happy. We love intensely, and we convince ourselves (or they convince us) that their lives and their happiness are somehow more important than our own. The reality is that no amount of sacrifice can make someone else happy. A person's happiness is a solo sport. If we're lucky, there is a support system around us as we individually heal our traumas, but ultimately, it is one person's very personal journey that they must decide to undertake.

I tried to follow through with my commitment but couldn't. I realized that I couldn't sacrifice my life. I realized it wasn't the right thing to do for my son, and it definitely wasn't the right thing to do for me.

Self-martyrdom, at least in this form, is never the right thing to do. After all the mistakes I'd made, it was now time to set an example for my son of someone who would fight for their own happiness. I'd wasted so much time already.

After telling my husband that we would no longer be together, I became a nightly recipient of his anger, blackmail, and verbal torture. He'd finally turned his darkness on me with great force and venom. I endured it for almost a year while I gathered enough resources and courage to officially end the marriage. In my soul, I knew I would get there. I knew I was moving in the right direction even though it hurt, and the process was long. It hurt me, and it hurt him.

Journal Break – Moment of Reflection

Your landscape may not be as dramatic or intense. Your experiences may have been even more traumatic. We are all presented with catalysts to transform our lives. What is the catalyst driving you? Describe your survival instinct, that part of you that is fighting to heal and grow and become your authentic self. My catalyst was the realization that if I didn't make the decision to end my marriage, I would be making the intentional decision to live a very miserable life. My survival instinct told me that I was deserving of happiness. It told me that I could make that a reality. My life was in my hands, and I would no longer abdicate that power to anyone else.

This is my landscape. It is the foundation of my negative thought patterns and limiting beliefs. I learned to not speak up for myself or value myself, and this created a persistent undercurrent of feeling unworthy. My experiences instilled in me a strong desire to be alone but also to accept the loneliness. I expected to be left or disliked. It created a fear of intimacy, of letting people become too close only to be hurt by them in the end. It caused me to be isolated even when surrounded by people.

Some people respond to painful experiences by being outwardly focused; my experiences made me retreat within. They are also the source of the various addictions I've carried with me—my addiction to food, to the wrong people, to martyrdom, to being so busy that I'm too tired to deal with my life or the people in it, an addiction to marijuana in my twenties and into my thirties, and other emotional crutches that showed up as guest stars on my path to wholeness.

What I've come to accept and realize is that you can't numb yourself out of feeling the most significant feelings that have shaped your life. I've tried, just as you might have tried or might still be trying. If so, you've probably discovered the cruel truth: when you try to numb yourself out of feelings, the numbing agent becomes less and less effective with each application. You'll need more things, more success, more food, more drugs, more sex, and more chaos to feel numb again. More, more, more until you wake up one day and realize that you aren't any more fulfilled and, in fact, you're running on empty.

No matter the intensity of the struggles you have faced, they provide benefits in the form of skills and abilities that allow you to transcend adversities. My stories/my landscape includes skills that I learned from my experiences. I was able to fine-tune my tenacity and patience, my ability to self-reflect and my interest in observing others. I developed a strong reliance on myself, along with the knowledge that when I put my energy into something, I can overcome and achieve what I set out to do. These experiences created in me a capacity for forgiveness. I could see that those closest to me were acting and reacting out of a deep hurt that I couldn't fully understand. Although I was sometimes a willing (and at times unwilling) recipient of their own self-hatred, I was not the source of their pain. By observing their pain, I could see it reflected in my own and know that I was responsible for my quality of life. My experiences made me stronger. They made me a fighter. They gave me confidence that, no matter what, I can take care of myself. They made me ambitious and resilient. They gave me a never-ending curiosity about human nature—questioning the motivations of why people do the things they do. I developed a deep compassion for people and an overwhelming desire to help them heal the wounds of their past and realize their own worth.

Every weakness I have has a corresponding strength that I developed to protect myself. Every strength has a shadow side weakness. The trick now (and the work we will do throughout this book and journey) is to unify these attributes so that we feel safe, empowered, strong, loved, lovable and confident.

We must be careful not to dwell on our wounds and our pain. We need to have thoughtful compassion for our own process and purposefully work to heal ourselves. We need to replace our negative thought patterns with positive, life-affirming thoughts and beliefs. *Our experiences are not our identities.* They are our lessons. We must learn our lessons and graduate to the next level of consciousness and well-being.

There are no quick fixes and no magic wands. No one else can or will do the work for you. If you want to turn into a butterfly, you need to put in the work.

I let you see my landscape. Are you ready to understand your own landscape and start forging your path to living your best life?

TIME WITH THE COACH:

1. What are the most defining experiences of your life? How do these experiences still affect you today?

When _____ happened, it made me feel _____. It still affects me today because ...

My example: When <u>I was kidnapped at nine years old,</u> it made me feel <u>isolated, lonely, betrayed, and angry</u>. It still affects me today through <u>my reluctance to get too close to anyone for fear of being hurt and betrayed.</u>

2. Who do you need to forgive, and for what?

3. What do you need to forgive yourself for, and why?

4. What weeds (negative thought patterns and unhealthy behaviors) did you develop during these experiences that still exist in your life? How do you see them holding you back from where you want to be?

5. What are the flowers (bright spots, positive relationships, or experiences) in your life? What gifts do you have in your life? What strengths did you develop because of these experiences? What important lessons have you learned that have helped you in other situations?

Create a Portfolio of Your Strengths

You've developed some incredible strengths along your journey. It is important to write these strengths down because the physical act of writing engages different parts of your brain than when you only think about them. Information becomes more engrained in your mind and works to reprogram it for positivity. It allows you to retain the good feelings you have about yourself. It will remind you of what you value about yourself, and it will also help regulate any negative emotions. You'll finally start to accept these positive attributes as truth. Come back to this list and add to it over time. Think back to when people have complimented you. There is no shame in acknowledging your strengths, so be shameless in listing and *owning* them. After all, you've earned them!

HONOR YOUR STORY MEDITATION

ESSENTIAL OILS

Essential oils recommendation: Frankincense allows you to let go of self-deception and reminds you that you are loved. Lemon oil allows you to stay grounded in the present moment and release fear and insecurity. Lavender calms insecurities that come from expressing your authentic self.

HONORING YOUR STORY MANTRA

I've survived challenging experiences, but these experiences do not define me.

HONOR YOUR STORY BREATHING TECHNIQUE

Place one hand on your chest and the other on your stomach.

Breathe as you normally would.

Notice as you continue to breathe if your belly or chest is rising with each inhale.

Gently guide yourself to a breathing pattern where your belly is rising with each inhale.

Concentrating on your belly, continue taking deep breaths.

Continue breathing this way for at least 15 breaths, more if you feel comfortable.

GUIDED MEDITATION

Sit in a comfortable position and begin by using the breathing technique above.

Do the full body scan relaxation technique:

Draw your attention to the top of your head, notice any sensations on your scalp, and relax your forehead, your eyebrows, and your eyes.

Continue to the back of your head and neck and release any tension you feel. Focus on your face, your cheeks, your mouth, your jaw, your chin. Let all the tension release from your face.

Continue breathing

Notice your shoulders and your arms. Let them drop naturally as the tension releases. Focus on your forearms and your elbows. Your wrists, hands, and fingers. Let all the tension go.

Focus on your chest. Relaxing and releasing here. Focus on your abdomen, releasing any tightness you feel.

Move to your hips and your pelvic area. Let the natural weight of your body allow you to sink even further here. Focus on your upper thighs, the backs of your legs and your knees. Feel the stress released.

Now release any tension you feel in your shins and your calves.

Focus on your ankles and the tops of your feet. Release and let go of any remaining tension you may feel. Now the bottoms of your feet and your toes,
you are now fully relaxed.

See yourself at the age you were when you experienced trauma.

See yourself just as you were at that age. See the innocence in your eyes.

Ask yourself, what does that child need from me now? Is it a hug? Is it reassurance that she'll be okay? Is it to be removed from that experience entirely?

Go to her. Give her exactly what she needs. Explain to her that she will not only survive these experiences, but she will also be triumphant.

Sit with her for a little while longer, continuing to provide her comfort and compassion.

As you and your younger self get ready to part ways, you both know that you can return to one another at any point for that mutual support, love, and compassion.

Breathe in the feelings of love, compassion, and wholeness.

Breathe out all the sadness and anger you've held onto for so long.

Repeat two more times.

As you come back to room awareness, slowly open your eyes. Give yourself a moment.

Take the time to write any notes about the thoughts or feelings that may have come up during your meditation.

A WALK-THROUGH NATURE

JACARANDA'S WISDOM

The Jacaranda Tree holds a special place in my life's journey. The Jacaranda symbolizes wisdom and rebirth. Each step along my path has been a rebirth and a coming home to myself.

The house that I was first brought home to on Los Padres Drive had a young Jacaranda tree that was small but mighty in the front yard. The majestic beauty displayed in her purple-blue trumpeted flowers awoke wonder and fascination in my child's mind. She was always there, a constant at my father's house when the chaos of my childhood pulled me in different directions.

As I got older, the Jacaranda held me in her canopy of complex leaf patterns, with each leaf held together by veins containing hundreds of micro-leaves. She provided the shade and shelter I craved. She grounded me as I stood beneath her branches and guided the cool breeze through my hair on scorching summer days.

When I came back to the house after my dad's passing, she welcomed me back like an old friend. She was older and wiser, as was I. She reminded me that shelter, protection, and wisdom were always available to me. I eventually needed to say goodbye to her at that house, but her presence continued to follow me.

She showed back up in abundance when I moved to a small rental house on a street that was famous for the canopies of hundred-year-old Jacarandas lining it. Artists and beauty-seekers visit at the peak of the trees' blooms to gaze at the branches stretching high into the sky and the blue-purple blooms reaching toward each other to create a vibrant tunnel.

And now, as I sit writing this, my very own Jacaranda sits in my front yard. This is my forever home. This is the place that I will hopefully leave to my son. I take from the Jacaranda the wisdom she continues to offer, but now I can reciprocate. I place the wisdom I've gathered along my journey at the base of her trunk as an offering to the Universe. The legacy of the Jacaranda will be passed down to my grandchildren so that they, too, can feel the wonder, beauty, majesty, wisdom, and rebirth she arouses in all who see her.

As you embark on this journey of rebirth and the search for inner truth, I invoke the wisdom of the Jacaranda as my gift to you.

Look back over your journey thus far. Is there a plant, tree, or flower that shows up time and again to remind you of who you are or where you came from? Maybe it's a body of water or the night sky. Perhaps it's an animal or bird that shows up when you need reassurance. It could be anything in the natural world that grounds you and brings you back to the core of who you are. Journal about the guides in the natural world that you've connected with over time. Research their spiritual meaning. This is nature's gift to you.

SECTION

Spring –Discover,
Unclutter, Cultivate

Spring – Discover, Unclutter, Cultivate

SPRING REPRESENTS NEW BEGINNINGS, rebirth, and rejuvenation. Just as we associate this time with cleaning our home after a long winter, it is also a time to clean and cultivate our minds and bodies. We begin the process of getting rid of the stale material and replacing it with new and vibrant life.

> "Sitting silently
> Doing Nothing
> Spring comes
> And the grass grows by itself."
> —Matsuo Basho

2.1 Releasing Limiting Beliefs and Self-Doubt

Our experiences and circumstances form the framework of who we have become. It has become our landscape. Etched in our minds are the views and beliefs we developed because of these experiences. Our beliefs hold the assumptions we've made about ourselves and our life. We created an understanding of how life is, how people act, and what we expect from the world. In some cases, these assumptions have been passed down through generations. Our current reality has been distorted by our past experiences. This is not our original programming. We are created for joy. Our blueprint at birth is designed for love and happiness.

It can feel like we are trapped by our circumstances and unable to make a move. It feels as if we have barbed wire wrapped around our arms, our legs, and our hearts. We've been trapped for so long that we stopped asking ourselves how we got here.

The barbed wire is the limiting beliefs we hold onto—about ourselves, about others, and about life. Now that you've explored some of the most significant experiences that shaped your life, beliefs, and behaviors, it's time to explore the remnants of those experiences. It is time to ask yourself, "How are those experiences still showing up in my life today?"

Memories of past experiences and our feelings about them keep us trapped and keep us small. They lead to the thoughts that we are less-than, unworthy, unlovable, not smart, too thin, too fat, not enough, or too much. It's not good to stay stuck in our wounds. We don't want to earn a Ph.D. in the field of our own (or anyone else's) *woundology*, but we also can't deny the wounds exist or the effects they have on our interactions with the world today.

Often there are two opposing thoughts in our heads. One tells us we need to try something new, explore our own healing, or take a chance. The other voice stops us, telling us it's not worth the effort; we won't be good enough; it will never work. One of those voices is the truth. The other one is telling us lies to keep us safe.

We are taught by the metaphysical text A *Course in Miracles* that there are only two sources of emotion: love and fear. All the wounds, hardships, and challenging experiences that remain with us are kept alive by our fear—either that something will happen to us again or that something will not happen at all.

How do we reconcile the fear of our desires not coming true and the fear of the possibility that they might come true? When you break free from the barbed wire, you may not exactly know what to do with yourself. Perhaps you are not even sure who you really are without those fears. You may feel that if you're set free from the fears that the wind can come along, and there is nothing holding you down. You feel free but unsafe, ungrounded, and unprotected from the coverage you used to have.

Your perception of reality has been skewed.

You had the perception that you were safe when you were tied up with barbed wire because the situation, no matter how painful, was familiar. Breaking free and making a change forces you to deal with the unknown and face the fear of uncertainty. You start to scare yourself out of the reality of what is by creating a nonreality of what hasn't occurred.

Those who have taken a risk in their life have found that once they acted, the situation or process wasn't as scary as their imagination made it out to be. It is so important to understand that the actions you take are not lifelong sentences. Every decision and every moment is transitional to the next. Permanence does not exist. Change is constant. The chance that you take and the change you make is only one stop along your journey.

The work is to understand our wounds and then get some distance from them, so we can release the control these events have over us, now and in the future. It's important to acknowledge and appreciate the journey and the insight gained. If we don't acknowledge the wound, it will keep on showing up in our lives in different and more impactful ways. Healing from past wounds takes work; however, it's time to recognize that your anger, sadness, resentment, or fear from the past is no longer serving you.

> "To plant a garden is to believe in tomorrow."
> —Audrey Hepburn

Journal Prompt

In what ways are you reliving past hurts in the present time? Do you pick the same relationships? Are you stuck in victimhood? Unaddressed emotions related to past wounds morph into the limiting beliefs we have about ourselves and our lives.

As a result of being abandoned as a child, then swiftly moved to a new school (School #2); another new school (School #3) in a different state; back to School #1 in California; and ultimately back to School #3—all within three years—I have a strong need for people to like me, to get along, or to not draw too much attention to myself. And, if people-pleasing does not work, just let me disappear. This has led me to not always stick up for myself in my adult life, as well as a real fear of success. One of my negative thought patterns is, "If I'm really successful, I won't be likable." I fear I'll be intimidating, or people will view me in a negative light.

The thoughts that get ingrained in us in childhood don't have to go through the "bullshit meter" that new thoughts and beliefs do. They are deep in our subconscious. We unconsciously factor these thoughts and beliefs into our daily decisions. Even when presented with the absurdity of these thoughts by our tribe of friends and loved ones, they don't go away. That happens only if and when we actively look at and counteract them. If you don't do the work, you run the risk of thinking that everything is under control, only to find that a random trigger brings you back to that fearful and unworthy place.

You need tools in your arsenal to combat these thoughts and get back to the reality of your greatness and get back to the real work of your life.

My limiting beliefs first showed up for me in a profound feeling of being unworthy. I didn't receive reassurance, love, or affection early in life. My basic needs, both emotional and physical, weren't a primary concern because my parents were deeply rooted in their own sadness, dysfunction, disappointment, and anger. As a result, I developed a deep sense that I did not matter, that my life didn't matter. This feeling perpetuated in a strong way until I was forty. Even now, I must be vigilant to ensure that I'm not overcome by it when I get triggered. Through my meditation practice and doing the exercises here, I've been able to develop an awareness of my thought patterns.

Limiting beliefs show up as that little voice that tells me I can't do something. It convinces me to eat healthily tomorrow. It will convince me that I won't be able to get that job I want or make that career shift I've been dreaming about or publish the book I've been formulating for decades.

It may show up for you in the behavior that picks a fight with your partner because you don't feel worthy of his/her love. It will be the thing that prevents you from reaching out to those who need your kind words because you feel like you can't really make a difference in someone else's life. It will show up in the habit of picking the wrong friends and partners who treat you poorly, shame you, ignore you, or abandon you—reaffirming the false thought that you are unlovable.

Your limiting belief shows up as fear and self-doubt. It mutes the inner voice that whispers to you about your passion and desires, which results in your belief that you have no purpose. The voice tells you that you'll never be creative enough or smart enough to achieve your dreams. It will tell you that someone else is so good at what you want to do that you shouldn't bother trying. Every time you decide to take a chance, one or more of your limiting beliefs may show up to convince you to play small.

Everything that your limiting beliefs are telling you is a lie. And they are not little white lies but bold-faced, ugly, mean lies. They were created to keep you safe from hurt or pain. But the unintended consequence is often a life only partially lived.

A limiting belief will continue to look for ways to reaffirm its truth until you are able to release that belief and replace it with a new empowering belief. Remember, these beliefs were created by your experiences, then were ingrained in your body, mind, and nervous system. It will take some work to confront what they have been telling you for the past ten to fifty years.

Journal Prompt:

Think about the different areas of your life: family and friends, health, career, money, physical environment, and romantic relationships. When do these limiting beliefs show up, and how can you spot them?

· Do your limiting beliefs show up in some of these areas? Maybe all these areas? In your journal, list areas where you know you're holding onto a limiting belief.

· Do your relationships reflect the long-held beliefs you've embraced about life? Describe how this shows up for you?

· Do you limit your career growth because you feel not good enough or smart enough, even though you have the training and experience necessary to do the job? Describe what you have stopped yourself from trying because of a limiting belief.

· Do you have people around you who add fuel to the negative thoughts you have about yourself? Do they sabotage your self-esteem to keep you small? How are they echoing the negative feelings that you have about yourself?

· How have you played small to support someone else's negative thought pattern or fears? Have you chosen to believe them or be influenced by their negativity? How has this relationship kept you from achieving your ambitions?

How can you really determine if a limiting belief is driving your behavior and keeping you stuck in a situation you so desperately want to change? The following list can help.

1. Regrets, limiting, or negative thoughts play in a loop in your mind. You can't control them or let them go.

2. You are overly critical, judging yourself and others.

3. You have a sense of entitlement, thinking that things should be given to you.

4. You feel like there will never be enough abundance or love for you.

5. You are stingy with your knowledge and your compassion.

6. You resent any competition.

7. You avoid taking risks.

8. You believe that the challenges you have just cannot be overcome.

9. You believe that people or situations can't change, so you think, "Why even try?"

10. You have a lot of excuses as to why you're not where you feel you ought to be. Everyone and everything else is to blame for where you are in your life.

11. You complain. A lot. About a lot of things.

12. You hang around with people who complain a lot.

13. You have unhealthy habits that either make you feel horrible about yourself through shame and regret, or these unhealthy habits keep you from making progress on your goals.

14. You obtain very little information before jumping to conclusions or making assumptions.

15. You can't articulate, admit, or express your fears to yourself or others.

16. You constantly question if you're doing the right thing or worry that you will fail miserably if you even try.

17. Worry consumes you. The worst-case scenario is always running through your head, and usually, it's the only outcome you consider.

18. Not only do you procrastinate, but you worry and stress about the impacts of your procrastination and worry about future procrastination.

19. Your feelings about wanting a perfect outcome prevent you from acting.

As you free yourself from the control of your own limiting beliefs, here are some of the ways your relationships may change:

1. As a result of no longer participating in someone else's cycle of negativity, they will have less control and influence over how you feel and what you choose to do. They may respond with an increasingly aggressive form of negativity as you no longer allow them to emotionally bully or manipulate you. This is their issue to resolve (or not)—not yours. You will no longer allow yourself to be emotionally blackmailed.

2. The energy that you've been supplying to them won't be generated any longer; they will have lost their audience and will stop their negative rhetoric, and/or they may find someone else to fuel their fires of self-hatred. Negativity and emotional manipulation require an audience to survive. Stop being someone else's audience, and they will naturally turn that energy elsewhere.

3. Your journey is fully supported. You may even inspire others to embark on their own healing journey. But it's important to note just because you're ready to go through this journey, others in your life may not be. And that is okay. Everyone needs to have the support and freedom to exist in this world in the way they want and need to. You only need the support of someone who wants to see you happy and whole.

It's time to imagine what your life would be if you lived without these limiting thoughts or, at the very least, turned their volume down low. It is important that you truly believe you are not only responsible for making the changes that need to be made in your life but are also undeniably able to make these changes.

It's time to get excited about the possibilities in your life. Go into this next exercise with an observant attitude and a curious mind. It helps if you are receptive, adaptive, and willing to entertain new and different perspectives.

TIME WITH THE COACH:

1. If you had freedom from this negative thought or behavior pattern, what would you have the confidence to try?

2. What goal would you like to achieve?

3. What is keeping you from achieving this goal?

4. What limiting belief(s) do you have about your ability to achieve this goal?

5. Are these limiting belief(s) true?

6. Are these beliefs rational? If so, what *evidence* (not feeling!) do you have that supports them?

7. When did you first come to believe these things? What was happening in your life at that time?

8. Do you have any evidence to disprove these beliefs?

9. Have these beliefs prevented you from achieving other goals? Where else in your life have they shown up?

10. How have these beliefs served you or protected you?

11. What are the consequences of *not* changing these beliefs? How will your life change or stay the same? How will you feel spiritually, emotionally, financially, or about your relationships?

12. How would you *feel* if you didn't believe these thoughts?

13. What is the exact opposite of your negative beliefs?

14. What's important about this time in your life that's making you consider this change?

15. If these limiting beliefs weren't holding you back, what else could you achieve in your life?

16. What would your life look like? What would change? What would you have more or less of in your life? How would you feel about yourself? What evidence do you have about this new positive version of these beliefs?

17. What habits or rituals would you need to implement to ensure progress toward your goals?

18. When can you commit to implementing these habits or rituals?

19. Can you find a role model who has achieved what you want to achieve? What can you learn from them?

20. Who can support you in your new belief(s)?

21. Create a mantra that you will repeat daily to reaffirm your belief in yourself. (Mine is, "Everything always works out for me.")

22. Reread Question #4 and your answer. Are these limiting belief(s) true?

RELEASING SELF-DOUBT MEDITATION

ESSENTIAL OILS

Essential Oils Recommendations: Lavender releases sadness and brings about a cleansing and harmonization of the mind, body, and spirit. Lemon washes away negativity and opens you up to new things in your life. Frankincense allows you to tap into your inner wisdom.

RELEASING SELF-DOUBT MANTRA

I'm able to release negative thought patterns and replace them with empowering beliefs about myself.

RELEASING SELF-DOUBT BREATHING TECHNIQUE

The Ujjayi Breathing is an excellent technique for bringing about a sense of calm and balance. Translated from Sanskrit, the definition of Ujjayi Breath is "the pranayama which gives freedom from bondage." We use this technique here to solidify the knowledge that you can achieve freedom from the fears and doubts that have plagued you.

Keeping your mouth closed, inhale and exhale while constricting your throat. Your breathing will sound slightly like snoring. Think Darth Vader. The inhale and exhale should be done for equal durations. Do this breathing technique for three to five minutes prior to the guided meditation

GUIDED MEDITATION

Find a comfortable sitting position. Make sure your spine is straight but not strained. Imagine a line coming from the top of your head up to the ceiling, pulling you straight and tall and confident.

Do a relaxing body scan (see Honor Your Story Meditation)

Think back to a time when you felt the most confident. Remember how strong you felt. Remember the internal power you possessed during that time.

Remember how you felt limitless and that you could do anything you set your mind to.

What were you doing? How did you look? How did you carry yourself?

Can you remember the thoughts you had at the time?

Let those positive feelings wash over you.

Know that you can tap into those feelings at any time. They are always available to you.

At your core, you are that same person—but even better now.

You have so much more knowledge and experience than you did then.

You are unstoppable.

Your success is inevitable.

Do three more cycles of the breathing technique.

As you come back to room awareness, slowly begin to open your eyes. Give yourself a moment.

Take the time to write any notes about what thoughts or feelings may have come up during your meditation.

2.2 Your Body – Cultivate Your Foundation

"It all begins with you. If you do not care for yourself, you will not be strong enough to take care of anything in life."—Leon Brown

Let's pause here for a moment. I want to congratulate you on doing some significant work. It's not easy to do the work you just did. It takes a lot of guts, vulnerability, and a desire to make progress in your life that is profound. And if you just reviewed the previous section or only partially did the work, that is ok. It's okay to take a break and go back to it. Either way—*You. Are. Amazing.* You are amazing for continuing the process and being dedicated to your own growth.

In this part of the journey, you will start to put more tools and techniques in your bag of tricks. These are things that will help you heal and give you the energy to continue your journey.

First things first—the foundation. Your body. I would personally love to live solely in a spiritual and mental state of being. I'm an introvert who loves time alone to read, learn, and reflect on all of life's complexities. I find solace and rejuvenation when I'm contemplating a hero's journey in a good biography, living in a fantasy world with works of non-fiction, learning about past life regressions and the *Journey of Souls*, brushing up on spiritual reflections and *Returning to Love*, or learning about self-development techniques and how to strive towards a *Daring Greatly* existence.

Sometimes you can find me hiding behind my introversion. It's my haven. I don't have to worry about being hurt, but mostly I don't have to worry about feeling uncomfortable around people. My introversion is my crutch. By focusing more intently on my mind and spirit, I often neglect the health of my body.

But that's not a balanced life. You need to have balance within the trinity—body, mind, and spirit. When one area is over or underdeveloped, there is an imbalance. You should not be totally physically focused and ignore the spiritual side of your existence. You should not put all your emphasis on mental pursuits and neglect the body. If you are ignoring any one part, you are likely overcompensating in another. Health or emotional problems are the consequence. Any imbalance creates unhealthy behaviors and unwanted outcomes.

Your body is the vehicle necessary to manifest your purpose and passion in this lifetime. It is critically important. You must care for your body for your entire life; at no time should you just throw in the towel. The effects of poor treatment on your body have a direct correlation with your ability to heal and grow emotionally. It has a direct influence on the energy you possess to achieve your goals. And it contributes to a high-functioning mind.

This is not something that is meant to stress you out by adding more things to your to-do list. When you create rituals, routines, and habits around these foundational activities, you won't have to stress or feel guilty about not having the ability to fit these healthy behaviors into your life.

If our life's trinity is body, mind, and spirit, then the body's trinity is sleep, nutrition, and body movement.

Sleep

You are on the journey to get back to your true nature. You cannot get there if you are exhausted. When lacking sleep, you not only get physically exhausted as your body craves rest, but you are also mentally exhausted and unable to think clearly. The chronically sleep-deprived are less alert and unable to concentrate. The ability to perform tasks requiring complex thought and logic is diminished.

As you work your way through this book, you will find areas where you don't need as much help. Pick up helpful tips and graduate to the next section. This is one of the areas where I excel. Sleep has never been one of my problems. Sure, I've experienced short periods of insomnia here and there, but if sleep were an Olympic sport, I would receive at least the silver medal. If I could get a job where the major qualification was napping, I'd be a star performer.

Some of the times that my sleep was interrupted the most was when I suffered from migraines. Out of a deep sleep, a migraine would jolt me awake and have me writhing in pain for hours until the medication kicked in. My migraines were caused by stress and often increased with frequency and intensity during times I was losing energy elsewhere in my life. I was paying attention to things that didn't need my attention, or I wasn't focusing my energy on the things that lifted my spirit. This knowledge is key; however, once a cycle of migraines came on, there was little else I could focus on because, in addition to rocking me with pain when the migraine was present, it completely zapped my energy for days. It's a cycle of lost energy. I lost my energy and focus, so the migraines came on. Once the migraines overtook my life, I couldn't focus on setting myself straight because not only was I exhausted, but I was also afraid to go to sleep every night, knowing how I would be painfully woken up in the middle of the night.

Anxiety and stress hit me the same way. When your subconscious mind is trying to reconcile all the worries you've pushed down during the day, you can wake up in the middle of the night with heart palpitations and a stream of thoughts about all the things you should be doing and all the things you shouldn't have done or said.

During these times, I used relaxation and meditation techniques to get me back on track. I also practiced some self-awareness by exploring the areas of my life where I was worried or stressed.

I wouldn't be able to untie the knots of crazy self-talk in my head or do the other things that I know are good for me and necessary to live a healthy life if I didn't sleep well. It's one of the foundational elements that need to be under control to start improving the quality of your life.

Sleep research and advice abound. There are countless articles and books that tell you what you need to do to improve the quality of your sleep. They fall just short of telling you the level of serial killer you will be if you routinely do not get enough sleep. Parents of newborns go a little insane until their little night owl gets a regular sleep routine.

The objective should be to get a solid 7-9 hours of sleep a night. Every night. As consistently as possible. I understand life gets in the way, but you need to protect your sleep like it's your job.

Shawn Stevenson wrote in *Sleep Smarter—21 Essential Strategies to Sleep Your Way to a Better Body, Better Health, and Bigger Success*, "Unless you give your body the right amount of sleep, you will never, I repeat, never, have the body and life you want to have."

When you don't get enough sleep, and you are chronically fatigued:

· Your brain is unable to repair nerve connections.

· You are unfocused during the day, making it difficult to hold onto information. You have a hard time learning new information because you can't focus. Productivity will decline.

· You have a higher probability of being emotionally exhausted. If you are under stress and fatigued, you may find it hard to keep a level head. You will be irritable and just generally in a bad mood.

· Your relationships may suffer, and parenting with patience will be even harder.

· You have poor judgment because exhausted people tend to ineffectively gauge the situation then apply the wrong behavior.

· Your body will produce more cortisol, the stress hormone. This effect tends to make you eat more and retain belly fat. Your thyroid will slow down, insulin isn't as effective, and your blood sugar levels can go crazy. Chronic sleep deprivation can increase your risk of more serious diseases like cancer, diabetes, and heart disease.

· Your body's natural repair system is not able to function properly. All living beings have a circadian rhythm. It's a 24-hour cycle of the physiological processes that occur in the human body. It's a timing system when hormones are released in your body and is how hormone production is regulated. Your body's repair processes happen during sleep. During sleep, growth hormones are released so that the body can maintain and repair muscle and decrease body fat. If you're not sleeping, your body is unable to repair itself to its full potential.

**When you DO get good sleep
(besides the opposite benefits of everything above):**

· It changes the cellular structure of the brain by providing a wash of cerebral spinal fluid. This process removes the damaging molecules associated with neurodegeneration. Your risk of chronic diseases and illnesses like heart disease, Alzheimer's, diabetes, and cancer will be reduced. Your risk of a stroke will decrease, as will immune system irregularities.

· It reduces inflammation and balances your hormones. Over time, with continued good rest, you will have decreased pain, better memory, you'll look younger, and have better skin. You'll be in better control of your emotions, and relationships won't suffer.

Here are some actions you can take to get better sleep

· Invest in a sleep tracker. Many devices that are used to track your physical activity can also track your sleep patterns. If you have trouble getting a good night's rest and you have an activity tracker, and yours doesn't track your sleep, it's time to upgrade. Monitor and track the duration and quality of your sleep. You may lie in bed for ten hours but only get a solid four hours of sleep. This is important knowledge to have so you know what actions you need to take.

· Establish a consistent routine. Going to bed and waking up at the same general time will help you get better sleep, even on the weekends.

· No ambient light. That means no phones, iPads or TVs in bed. If you need time in bed to wind down, read an actual book. You know, the paper kind.

· Limit alcohol consumption and stop eating three hours before bedtime.

· If you take naps and can't sleep at night. Stop taking naps or limit them to no later than 3:00 p.m. and no longer than 20 minutes.

· Do not be a clock watcher. If you wake up frequently during the night, turn your clock face away from your line of vision, don't wear a watch to bed, and keep your cell phone out of the bedroom. This activates brain activity and makes it harder to fall back asleep. You'll wake up your brain doing the math of how little sleep you've gotten and how much time you have left to get rest. Remove the clock if you can't help yourself.

· Make your bedroom and bed comfortable. If you're sleeping on a sagging mattress or your pillows are flat, invest in some new bedding. If you suffer from back pain, try using a pillow between your knees or somewhere around your legs. Keep your bedroom dark and cool. It's hard to fall asleep and stay asleep when you are too warm. Our bodies are tuned to darkness. This means that trying to sleep when there is a lot of light will increase your state of alertness and reduce the quality of sleep.

· Make your bed dedicated to sleep and sex. Maybe a little light reading. Don't work, eat, drink, or multi-task in the bedroom.

· Watch for hidden caffeine in your food or other drinks.

· Keep a pad and paper next to your bed to make lists of tasks that keep your brain from resting.

· Exercise regularly. Working out helps you sleep better as your body repairs itself. Just don't do it too close to bedtime. It could prevent you from falling asleep.

· If you wake up in the middle of the night for a trip to the bathroom, consider limiting your liquid intake before bed. Getting back to sleep can be difficult.

· If you wake up in the middle of the night and cannot fall back to sleep within 10-15 minutes. Get up and find a chair with low lighting. Try coloring, meditate or simple word search books. Do not read or use computers, cellphones or watch TV. You want to keep your brain from becoming overstimulated.

· If you need help falling asleep, consider taking a bath before bed. Use Epsom salts and lavender oil to reduce stress and anxiety and wash the day away. Use a relaxation meditation for sleep when you get into bed.

· Avoid sleep medications if you can. It's better to exhaust all possible solutions before turning to meds.

· If you are chronically sleep-deprived and you have tried everything, go see a doctor. Something else might be going on. Check out every possible cause and solution.

Now that you know the effects sleep has on you and your body and some tools to improve your sleep let's explore motivation and barriers to focus on good sleep. I imagine the information here are reminders. You've heard this advice before. You may already know *what* to do, so the question now may be—why haven't you taken the necessary action to improve your sleep?

TIME WITH THE COACH:

List all the areas in your life that would improve and the things you could accomplish or be more effective at if you were well-rested and had more energy.:

· What are you prioritizing over your sleep? And why?

· What changes do you need to make in your schedule or routine to prioritize good sleep?

- When can you commit to making these changes?

Create a Sleep Routine to Prioritize Sleep

Creating a bedtime routine will help you start to separate the bustle of the day from the calm that is needed to rest and recharge. If you struggle with letting go of the events of the day, create a powerful routine that transitions you from day to night to support better sleep.

After a storm passes, there begins the period of recovery and tranquility. Humans are no different. Our bodies and our minds need a period of sleep to prepare themselves for what's to come the next day.

Starting three hours before your ideal bedtime to three hours after you wake up, write your pre- & post-sleep schedule. Create what your ideal schedule should be to prioritize sleep.

With the first exercise, you explored your motivation to make sleep a priority. If you are one of the many people who think that you'll lose out or waste precious time sleeping, you can now see that getting good sleep will help you be more effective at what you're doing and accomplish more.

You then explored what you're prioritizing over getting good sleep. Perhaps it's a fear of missing out. Maybe you're obsessed with ensuring all the little things around the house get done. Maybe you're too dedicated to your favorite TV show. It's time to start re-prioritizing your life to see what you can let go of and shift around, so your sleep isn't interrupted.

Next, you were asked to specifically identify what changes you need to make to prioritize sleep. Nothing in this guide will work unless you take specific action. Set your intention, act, and see results.

Finally, you were asked to make an evening and morning schedule. This is the schedule you will stick to most days. Sticking to a schedule will help regulate your system and will give you back that energy you have been missing.

Good night!!

Body Image

My body has been the holding place for all my insecurities and self-doubt. I fear it is similar for most women. It played the role of protector from pain while also being an obvious reflection of that pain. The journey to body positivity will likely be a lifelong issue—one that will remain on my watch-list.

When I was five, a family member casually said that I had "thunder thighs," imprinting on my psyche that something was wrong with my body. By the time I was seven, I was using food as comfort and developed the skill of sneaking and hiding food. Food is my first thought when I need comfort. It is my reason and my excuse. It allowed me to play small, no matter how big I got. Food has been my protector, my friend, my enemy, and my companion. It shows up for all occasions—when I'm lonely, scared, stressed, or exhausted. When I had the desire to disappear, the inside of a potato chip bag was my hiding place. It has always been available to me. The fact that it, in the end, does not provide me any comfort for those emotions is a minor detail, not a deterrent.

My appreciation for my body has grown (and sometimes waned) over the years. Most of the time, I'm able to maintain deep appreciation and gratitude for what my body can do. It is, however, a relationship that I must nurture with intention and continue the work to maintain a healthy relationship.

We all deserve to have autonomy over our own bodies, and that means stopping the war on our bodies. Diet culture takes the most vulnerable feelings we have about ourselves and manipulates them for profit. It's time for a peace treaty where we honor our bodies. We need to do what feels right for our bodies, no matter the size or shape, and stop doing the things that make us feel bad about ourselves.

If we only had to fight against our own inner demons related to our body image, we might be more effective at developing healthier relationships faster. We must contend with the media, which plays evil, evil games with our self-perception. Telling us what perfection is and how we can easily attain that perfection—for a few hundred dollars. When big media stars make appearances with an 18-inch waist, it's hard not to covet that look and lifestyle. When makeup lines create products that cover up every single feature of your face that makes you unique and beautiful, it makes growing old naturally an impossibility. The journey to love yourself lasts a lifetime. Be vigilant and fight against the countless daily messages that tell you that you are not good enough, you're not skinny enough, your nose is the wrong shape and countless other messages created to sell products.

The actions we take inform how we feel. To build a better image of our bodies, follow these tips to honor your body and combat the forces that lead you astray from healthy thoughts and behaviors.

1. Dress for the body you have, not the body you wish you had. It is self-imposed torture to be carrying around a pair of jeans that fit you six years ago. You are still holding onto them because you just know you're going to fit into them one day. There is no shortage of denim (or other fabrics that I know of). You can buy and wear jeans that fit. Dr. Pat Allen says, "Women need to feel good to do good." You need to start feeling good (and authentic) in your appearance. Strive to look and feel your best right now, not ten pounds from now. Get rid of the clothes that do not fit you, whether they are too big or too small.

2. Avoid the countless messages and commercials whose only goal is to take your money. Stop buying fashion magazines, unfollow or scroll past unattainable images, and stop watching TV geared to make you feel so bad that you'll pay any amount of money to fix what they say is wrong with you. Do not click on the hateful, misogynistic "news" stories about celebrities without makeup or celebrities who have lost weight or gained weight. These stories are not newsworthy and were created to be a mind-fuck to make you feel bad about yourself and spend money.

3. Appreciate your body. If you have strong legs (or "thunder thighs" like mine), appreciate them, no matter what size they are. Love and appreciate the things about your body that are glorious and beautiful.

4. Gently challenge yourself physically. Climb, run, walk, squat, do yoga—something that you had in your mind you could not do. Appreciate the strength and vitality of your body. *Live* in your body. Connect with your body in more and more physical ways. Feel your muscles. Having muscle fatigue from a good workout is a great feeling.

5. Try to make food decisions based on the benefits it provides to your body. Nourish your body. Give it what it needs to function at its best.

6. Enjoy the foods that you so diligently restrict yourself from eating. Life is not an either/or proposition – in anything. Especially food. Life is built on a both/and equation. You can both nourish your body most of the time and enjoy the foods you want to.

7. Practice mindful eating. Turn off the TV, sit at the kitchen table and just focus on the food you are eating.

8. Get rid of the guilt. Guilt over food is pointless and detrimental. If you over-indulge, just commit to also nourishing your body with healthy foods.

9. As you're growing to respect your body more and more, make sure you don't let anyone else disrespect it. Allowing others to criticize your body is the ultimate act of self-hatred. We can be awful to ourselves, but once we

allow someone else to be critical in a harmful way, we are compounding the abuse.

10. Eliminate the scale if it is torturing you. Keep it if it helps you but get real with your relationship with the numbers. Body weight fluctuates so much in either direction based on water, elimination, time of the month, age and other things going on with your body. It's not an accurate reflection of health and vitality. Try to use the fit of your clothes as a gauge. Better yet, let how you *feel* be your gauge.

11. And finally, get real with yourself about your thoughts on your body image. Introduce self-compassion into your thought process. If you are engaging in behaviors that make you feel shame or self-loathing, seek professional help. Life is too short, and you are too valuable to have your life consumed with negative feelings about yourself.

TIME WITH THE COACH:

· What is the earliest memory you have of your body? What positive and negative messages did you receive that informed how you now feel about your body?

· What current behaviors, thoughts or activities make you feel bad about your body or how you look?

· What current behaviors, thoughts, or activities make you feel good about your body and how you look?

· What insecurities, fears or trauma lead you to think or treat your body poorly? Where did you first hear these messages?

- What assumptions do you have about your body? For example, "I will not be likable if I'm thin," or "If I stop obsessing about food and exercise, I will lose all control and gain a lot of weight." What is the source of this belief? Is this belief true? What thought can replace this belief?

List at least ten things that you love about your body. What are your favorite features? When do you feel good in your body?

Describe a time when were you most accepting of your body?

What daily action or activity can I do that honors my body?

Nutrition

My primary drug of choice has always been food. It is my Achilles heel, my weak spot. It's the place where my insecurities and demons manifest themselves most. It's the addiction I come back to, to keep myself overweight enough to disappear, push people away, and fulfill the prophecy that I'm not worthy. Because, of course, only thin people are worthy of goodness in this world.

What can I tell you about nutrition when it's the place that I struggle the most? I can tell you what I know from being in the trenches; I have had struggles. It's the game in life that I will never stop playing. I'm always on the line taking the hit on this one. I do what I always do with any topic that intrigues or challenges me. I research it. I learn about it. From every angle.

What I can tell you is that whether you have a problem with food or not, it's still one of the most important things to understand about your physical health—the way food affects the body.

From Paleo to Veganism and everywhere in between, your goal should be to find a combination of solutions that work for you. Do your own research and understand how foods affect your mind and body and make the choices (most of the time) that support a disease-free body.

God's Green Earth (GGE) was born out of a conversation with a friend who has a healthy relationship with food. She told me she doesn't worry about calories or health benefits if the food source is from GGE. She made this statement years before the Paleo movement exploded and the gluten-free trends started. She said it when I was still marveling and envious of a friend's ability to eat only a sliver of pizza and a small bag of peanut M&Ms all day, wishing I had her willpower and skinny waist. If the food is not GGE, if it requires a factory to get it to your table, then you need to reconsider if you should be eating it at all. At the very least, evaluate how much of these processed foods you allow into your diet.

But this is easier said than done. Convenience and cost are big factors. It is easier to prepare boxed and canned foods that have been manufactured to make your life easier (and sell more products). Strive to incorporate more GGE fresh food. Find a balance that doesn't make you crazy.

Do your own research so that you can make your own informed decisions about what to put in your body. Here are some of my favorite books and research to help you on your journey.

The reason why you have a hard time resisting your favorite manufactured food is not a mystery, and it's not simply a lack of willpower. You may be the *user*, but the food producers are the *pushers*. They manufacture food to be addictive so that you'll buy more and more of them. Vani Hari is the "Food Babe" who is a crusader to uncover the secrets of what is in our food supply. Her website, Foodbabe.com, exposes the harmful chemicals food manufacturers use—and we consume. She points to the corporate/financial link that these manufacturers have with media to promote these manufactured, disease-causing foods through "best diet" lists and other non-traditional forms of promotion.

Kelly Brogan, M.D.'s book A *Mind of Your Own*, talks about reframing traditional treatments for depression. Her research has led to the conclusion that "our health is being outpaced by lifestyles that are not aligned with how we are biologically designed to live." She goes on to say that "we eat foods that are unrecognizable to our systems, and we expose ourselves to environmental factors that assault our cells."

What does all this mean? It means that our bodies are not biologically capable of breaking down some of the things that we ingest (the food we eat or the polluted air we breathe). Eating manufactured foods creates damage to our bodies and our cellular structures. It impacts how our complex body systems work, ultimately causing inflammation.

Inflammation is your body's natural reaction when it needs healing. Think of a sprained ankle, a cut, or a bruise. The body detects a need to defend itself against something harmful and swelling results. This is what happens in your gut when you eat processed foods. Your body identifies these things as toxic. Your body reacts by creating inflammation which then starts to breakdown your intestinal lining. Undigested food particles and bacteria seep into the blood stream. This is what is called a *leaky gut*. This cell debris affects how your entire body and brain perform. The primary causes of a leaky gut are sugars, grains, gluten, processed foods, preservatives, and refined flour.

With continued use of these substances, our bodies develop chronic inflammation. Chronic inflammation is one of the primary causes of diseases. If increasing your risk of cancer, dementia, heart disease, seizures, headaches, diabetes, and more isn't enough to convince you to stay away from these types of foods, you will also increase your risk of depression, obesity, brain fog, insomnia, lethargy, and more.

One of my favorite discoveries into the science and medical impacts of food has been from Dr. Steven Gundry. Dr. Gundry's mission is to "dramatically improve human health, happiness, and longevity through (his) unique vision of diet and nutrition." Having 30 years of experience as a cardiothoracic surgeon, his philosophy has been well-researched and documented. His approach focuses on maintaining good gut health by eliminating bad gut bacteria and replacing them with good bacteria.

As I've struggled with food, body image, and weight issues for most of my life, I simply wanted to find some sort of solution that allowed me to not obsess over food for most hours of the day. Thinking about what I should eat, what I shouldn't eat, guilt, regret, and self-hatred swirled in my head on a loop. It has been all-consuming and torturous for most of my life. I desire not to have a mind controlled by food.

Gluten. Studies have shown that gluten causes inflammation. Even if you are not overly sensitive like those who suffer from Celiac Disease, gluten still has a big impact on your health. Gluten is the sticky stuff in your food. In Latin, it literally means *glue*. Think about the sticky stuff left in the strainer after you drain pasta. This gluey substance interferes with the breakdown and absorption of nutrients, resulting in poorly digested food. When your food is not digested all the way, your body sends out a signal like an alarm to the immune system. The immune system gets to work and starts attacking the small intestines, causing inflammation. This creates an opening in the small intestines where toxins start leaking into your cells and your blood stream. Even if you do not feel sick with stomach problems, this phenomenon is still happening. The toxic particles enter your cells, and the contaminated cells travel to the brain – causing inflammation. This can result in depression, seizures, migraines and headaches, anxiety, ADHD symptoms and nerve damage.

Dairy. Dairy acts like morphine to the body. It signals the opiate receptors in the brain and in the body. A lot of people have sensitivities to dairy products. I'm allergic to milk and am proof positive that you can indeed live without it. To see if you have any dairy sensitivities, remove all dairy from your diet for 30 days. Slowly reintroduce dairy products, one at a time. With each new dairy product introduced, be mindful of how your body feels.

Sugar (real or artificial). Sugar intake has been scientifically linked to cardiovascular diseases, impacts your liver, causes inflammation, and has a host of other physical effects. Artificial sweeteners like those in the little packets or contained in your diet drinks have no calories – which is one of the reasons your body cannot digest them. They are insulin resistant, still contribute to diabetes and cause weight gain. There is no benefit whatsoever to having this in your diet. Be a religious label reader. Anything with sugar or a word ending in "-ose" should be reconsidered.

GMO Crops. Genetically Modified Organisms. These are the pesticides and toxins put on crops such as soy, canola, and corn. According to some reports, 80% of processed foods contain GMOs. On a trip back to the Midwest (the corn and soy capital of the US), I drove past field after field. All the fields had these huge wings of pesticide sprayers. The scientific community still does not know all the impacts GMOs and other pesticides have on the human body. All I know is that I do not want to continue to be a science experiment.

Some studies have linked GMOs to food allergies, infertility, toxic effects on our kidneys and livers, birth defects and cancer. Countries outside of the United States have banned GMOs in their food (parts of Europe, Australia, Japan, and dozens of other countries) or must clearly label GMOs on food packages. I don't know the extent of the political and financial connection in the US, but this stuff is big business. And big business is being prioritized over the health and well-being of its citizens.

Eating clean is not easy, nor is it effortless. Find communities with likeminded people. The Plant Paradox/lectin-free community is growing. You can find them all over your favorite social channels. One of my favorite resources is Bobby Parrish. He, along with his wife and collaborators, manages the Flavcity brand. He is dedicated to many of these clean eating approaches. He has an app where you can scan food to see if it is "Bobby-approved." He's making it easier for people to identify the hidden ingredients that are not good for us. You can find him home cooking, shopping at all the major food stores, providing recipes, and showing how you can incorporate food alternatives at a reasonable price.

Nature's foremost gift to us is sustenance. She provides us with healing fruits, vegetables, herbs, nuts, seeds, and more. In the book *The Green Which*, Arin Murphy-Hiscock said, "All fruit carries seeds, which are the beginning of life." In this book, the author describes the magical qualities connected to fruit. The healing powers of all nature's gifts have been well documented. Incorporating more of what nature offers in the most natural state possible serves to protect us from a myriad of preventable diseases.

I grew up in a time when, if we had a vegetable that wasn't a potato (hello, Mid-West comfort food), it typically came from a can. Canned corn (really a grain) and canned green beans were the staples. The journey back to vegetables has been a winding road. I've had to learn what real vegetables taste like. Canned spinach (shudder) is nothing like the fresh stuff. I hated canned asparagus. But now, fresh asparagus is one of my favorites. You must cook them correctly, or they become mush. Also, a learning process. My brother and I still argue about his vegetable-avoidance tendencies. Consuming them closest to their natural form will allow you to fully accept the gifts and benefits that nature provides.

TIME WITH THE COACH:

The following questions and statements are for you to simply create awareness around your food and nutrition thoughts and beliefs. Pay attention to the questions that elicit the biggest reaction. The concepts that you identify most with will be the areas to keep on your watch-list and continue to explore ways to create a more powerful mindset around.

· I have a healthy relationship with food.

· Typically, when I eat, I do it:

o Thoughtfully and intuitively

- o Mindlessly

- o Obsessively

· I enjoy eating. T or F

· I eat when I'm hungry. T or F

· I enjoy food. T or F

· My diet is balanced with a variety of foods. T or F

· I stop eating when I feel satisfied. T or F

· I'm afraid of feeling hungry. T or F

· I'm eternally on a diet.   T or F

· I go for long periods of time without eating, or I skip meals. T or F

· I eat for fuel, not to suppress my emotions. T or F

· Thoughts of food interfere with my daily life. T or F

· I frequently compare what I eat and my body to others. T or F

· I find it difficult to make healthy food choices. T or F

· I feel shame or guilt when I eat certain foods. T or F

Journal Prompt

· My life has been impacted by food issues in the following ways:

- Describe in detail your current beliefs and relationship with food and nutrition.

- What discoveries did you make in this section about your relationship to food and body image?

- Given your answers to the questions above, what small changes can you commit to that will improve your relationship with food?

Physical Movement

All your physical demands need to be met. We've talked about sleep and nutrition. Moving your body is the final pillar to creating a strong foundation. Consistently moving your body is so important. If you already have exercise established as a habit in your busy life, that works for you—fantastic. For a great many of us, it's hard to get started and then even more difficult to maintain a consistent exercise habit over time. Those of us who have a hard time being consistent find it's usually the first thing we give up when our daily schedules start to squeeze in around us.

Getting and staying physically healthy should be a priority. Your body is your vehicle to manifest your dreams and desires in this lifetime, and your vehicle needs rest, proper fuel, and tuning up. Losing weight or getting in shape is 80% dependent on the food you eat. Only 20% of weight loss is controlled by exercise. Therefore, the motivation to get moving needs to come from the other benefits received because of exercising.

Disease prevention and brain health are the top reasons why you need to start moving on a regular basis. Our bodies are designed for movement. A common belief is that our strength is reduced, and we lose balance as we grow older. The truth is we lose balance and strength from not moving enough as we get older. As our lives become more sedentary, our muscle strength weakens.

It's not just our physical body that benefits from regular exercise. Studies have shown that regular exercise has a positive impact on our brains. Our brains use more energy than any other organ. Your heart is the biggest generator of electromagnet energy. Therefore, when you increase your heart rate through exercise, it generates energy that can then be used by the brain. Studies have shown when you exercise, your focus, concentration, and ability to learn and remember all increase. It is just a fact: exercise makes you smarter.

My relationship with exercise has been complicated. I'm not coordinated or flexible. I'm not light on my feet, nor am I delicate or graceful. When I walk, I pound the pavement rather than glide. Maybe because of the pounding, I have aches in my joints and my knees, making exercise often uncomfortable. Consequently, I have consistently exercised on an inconsistent basis for the last twenty years. I'll go through long stretches (years) where I'm full-out exercising. I've belonged to large fitness studios, and to a CrossFit gym for three years. When I was pushing myself and working hard, I felt fantastic. Then I'll have the times of limited exercise.

I had a love/hate relationship with CrossFit. I loved the weights, the barbells, the Olympic lifts and feeling strong. I didn't love all the focused attention on me to compete and complete the workout of the day (WOD). I loved how I felt afterward because I knew I had just completed a workout where I pushed myself past my mental and physical limits. I hated the injuries and tendonitis in my shoulders that prevented me from lifting my arms over my head toward the end. I loved the comradery and support, but I hated the fear that the workout of the day would require running (my least favorite form of exercise). I cannot regulate my breath correctly, and my knees don't like it either.

CrossFit made me burned out and injured. I quit and bought some home workout equipment. And I have been consistently inconsistent in using it ever since. I'm not able to push myself in the same way. What worked about CrossFit was needing to be there at a certain time for class. No matter what, if you showed up, you were doing the workout. I was pushed and supported. It was a community. Most of the time walked away from class feeling strong and like a bad ass for having completed the WOD.

I've done yoga; however, after hurting my back, some poses and stretches are not ideal. I can still do balance poses like nobody's business.

The aim is to become more active and find that balance between what you like to do and developing the discipline to do it consistently. If you are resistant to establishing an exercise routine, the key is to make it easy and fast, with a compelling reason why you should exercise.

Make sure that when you do start moving with more frequency and intensity, you pay attention to how you are feeling. It is okay to have muscle soreness. It's normal, and it means that your muscles are getting stronger. You will *want* to feel some soreness occasionally. You also need to honor how your body is feeling. Take rest days as needed. Push yourself but do not injure yourself. Seek the advice of your doctors.

Be creative in incorporating movement. Not all activity needs to be done at the gym or with gym equipment. Go outside and explore. Find walking paths or hiking trails. Go dancing. Play.

TIME WITH THE COACH:

· What physical activities did you love doing as a child?

· Are your other physical needs being met? Sleep? Nutrition?

· What time of day do you find it easiest to exercise and why?

· What activities make you feel strong and capable when you do them?

· Make a list of what gets in the way of prioritizing movement each day.

· For each of the barriers you identified, what strategies can you employ to overcome them?

· If you haven't exercised in some time, what small activities can you do to increase your movement and mobility?

· What triggers or enablers can you use to remind and encourage you to move? (Set up a time with a friend to walk, put your athletic shoes and clothes out, etc.)

Self-Care Assessment

When you feel your energy depleted, use this assessment to understand where you need to focus additional attention to ensure a strong and vibrant foundation.

Self-Care Quick Quiz

· I appreciate my body and all that it can do.

· I am well hydrated.

· I am maintaining a regular meditation practice.

· I have eaten something nutritious in the last three hours (or your last meal if it's early morning).

· I have stretched and moved my body today.

· On average, I sleep 7-8 hours a night.

· I have not done a quick weight loss/fad diet in the past six months.

YOUR FOUNDATION MEDITATION

ESSENTIAL OILS

The following essential oils are associated with health and strength. Peppermint will give you a boost of energy. Ancient Greeks used thyme to signify courage. Eucalyptus supports your immune system and increases respiratory health. It reduces joint and muscle pain. Pine also provides relief for muscle and joint paint as well as helps with fatigue.

YOUR FOUNDATION MANTRA

I honor my body. I am worthy of having good health and vitality.

YOUR FOUNDATION BREATHING TECHNIQUE

Use the Bhastrika breathing technique to create strength in your body and mind. This breathing technique produces heat in the body and stimulates the metabolic rate.

Sit tall and relax your shoulders. Take 2-3 deep cleansing breaths through your nose, expanding your belly and fully expelling the air on the out-breath.

After the third inhale, forcefully expel the air through your nose. Your next in-breath should be forcefully taken in. Do this rapid and forceful breathing for 10 breaths. If you feel comfortable, continue to the next round of 20 breaths. Over time, and as you feel more comfortable with the technique, work up to doing three rounds. Round 1—10 breaths; Round 2—20 breaths; Round 3—30 breaths.

YOUR FOUNDATION MEDIATION

Find a safe, flat-surfaced walking path (maybe in backyard or a nearby park).

Today's meditation will be a walking meditation while witnessing the natural rhythm of your breath.

Do this meditation without headphones

Focus on the oxygen entering your body and how your body naturally releases the breath. Focus on the movement of your legs and your arms. Try adjusting the speed at which you walk (faster or slower) until you find a calming pace that feels right for you.

Continue this walking meditation for at least 15 minutes.

When you are done, find a comfortable place to sit. If you're out during the day, feel the sun on your face. Just for a few moments, direct your attention to how your legs feel. Feel the warmth of your warmed muscles.

Notice your heart. It works hard to pump blood through your body.

Notice your lungs. Refreshed with the constant flow of oxygen in and out.

Now give your body all your gratitude for what it can accomplish FOR you.

The complex systems and workings of the human body are miraculous.

As you come back to awareness, slowly begin to open your eyes. Give yourself a moment.

Take the time to write any notes about what thoughts or feelings may have come up during your meditation

A WALK-THROUGH NATURE

THE INATTENTIVE GARDENER

I'm not always the most attentive gardener. In fact, my ability to ignore the invasion of weeds is profound. Sometimes the work feels too overwhelming. Weeding is not something that you can do once, and you're free from their aggression forever. It takes constant attention and observation to make sure the insidious plants aren't overrunning your garden.

I was living in a small rental house in the final stages of my marriage. There was a small patch of dirt where I would try to grow flowers and other plants. Try as I might, I couldn't control the weeds that would invade the space. The combination of the overwhelm in my personal life and the overwhelm of the weeds in the garden was more than I could bear. I was unable to control very little in my life and spending energy taming the weeds was not a priority.

The attributes of weeds mirror the attributes of our lingering fears in the form of our limiting beliefs. The longevity of a weed seed is long—as are the fears that were planted in our childhood. Weeds are adaptive. They can change and morph to adjust to their environment. As our lives continue through the various stages, we carry with us our limiting beliefs. They tend to adjust and take root in our new circumstances. Weeds reduce the quality of our plants and crops. They attract diseases and other invaders like insects. Typically, our fears attract others to us who mirror or even amplify our own. Weeds steal nutrients, sunlight, and water from neighboring plants. Our fears, left untended, will steal our energy, joy, and potential.

Starting the process to eliminate the limiting beliefs that hold us back is like weeding a garden. You can't have a beautiful garden *and* let the weeds go unchecked. You can't have a beautiful life without looking at how these disempowering beliefs show up.

Removing weeds without toxins (like our own addictions) requires us to get our hands dirty. It requires us to dig deep into the soil and slowly and patiently pull out the root. Cutting them back will not excavate the source of the problem.

The healing process begins with the identification and excavation of the weeds we've carried with us. It's not an easy journey, nor is it a fast one. But it's one that pays dividends in the form of living a purposeful life that feels and looks good.

Visit a nearby garden. Imagine the care and attention that the groundkeepers must dedicate to making the beautiful landscape. Understand that your soul is not very different than the most attractive plant that you're drawn to in that garden. Realize that you have the ability to bloom just as vibrantly.

SECTION

Summer – Feed,
Nurture, Blossom

Summer – Feed, Nurture, Blossom

IN SUMMER, THE DAYS get longer, and the sun shines brighter, giving needed energy and life to all living things. In the light, we find our joy, our essence. We're able to see more clearly through the challenging times we've experienced. We start to awaken to the beauty and nourishment life and nature can provide.

Colors are brighter, and plants flourish and blossom. Trees are bearing fruit. It's a time to continue planting summer crops so the fruit can be harvested for the winter.

As we progress on this journey, we'll use summer as our inspiration to continue our growth, focusing our energy on settling into the fact of what we now know: we are worthy and capable of living the life we were meant to live. Let's take advantage of the extended light given to us to expand our spirits and our minds as we start to open to new, empowering possibilities

3.1 Powerful Thinking

I had a CrossFit coach who would always tell me as I was struggling to get through the workout (which was every workout), "You gotta get your mind right." He was so right. Once you have your foundation established (good sleep, nutrition, and exercise), it's time to ensure your mindset is as powerful as it can be and steadfastly believes in your ability to achieve your goals. Maintaining the ability to believe that you are capable and worthy of having a successful and joyful life, even amid life's challenges and adversities, is a vital piece of your overall wellness.

The way the mind works is complicated. We discussed limiting beliefs in the previous section and how past experiences and fears can be locked in your mind and cause you to be a prisoner of your negative thought patterns. It takes a concerted effort to understand how your thought processes are working and holding you back.

We'll dive deeper here to start to make the shift from a mind that is locked in a cycle of negative thinking and emerge with a powerful mindset that *knows* that living a good and healthy life is your birthright.

Powerful thinking is not the ability to force yourself to think positively. Any type of advice that tries to force positive thinking over doing the work to create a powerful mindset is toxic. Positive thinking alone may present a mere moment of relief from a negative thought pattern, but without the skills you'll learn here to systematically create a powerful mindset with tools you can return to, you will only find temporary relief. You may find yourself "white-knuckling" in a painful situation. Power denotes the ability to be resilient and use that strength when needed to make a shift in thinking, but also the power to feel the hard and painful feelings when needed.

Powerful thinking is understanding that we are not immune to succumbing to the natural ebbs and flows of the effects of life on our mental wellbeing. Powerful thinking allows us, when we're ready, whether through our own efforts or seeking the assistance of qualified help, to bounce back to a place of having a strong mindset. This does not in any way minimize the challenges of those dealing with neurodiversity or other mental health concerns. Our brains are complex organs. Leaving no stone unturned to achieve a mindset that truly believes in your own capabilities and self-worth is the goalpost.

When you have dominion over your own thought processes, you can pause at a thought and determine if that thought is true or not. For instance, if your thought patterns continually repeat that you're not good enough, the ability to think powerfully will enable you to first recognize that the thought exists (instead of just making you feel horrible and not understanding why), then critically question if that thought is true and serving your higher good. Powerful thinking allows you to observe the impact others have on your ability to think good thoughts. When you are no longer controlled or manipulated by your own negative thinking created by past trauma, and you can recognize the negative impact of others' behaviors on your experience, you have successfully developed powerful thinking.

3.2 Cultivating Awareness

Our overall wellbeing requires us to develop the skill of awareness. Life strategies and techniques are required to become more aware of when that negative mindset is present and how to shift your focus. First and foremost, you need to gain awareness of the patterns of your thoughts.

We live on an information superhighway. It comes at us from so many different directions. The highway is jammed. Horns are honking in every direction, trying to get our attention, our reaction, and often our money. Words and images are on a constant feed. There are no more traffic signs and very few rules of the road. The information presented can be real or fake and is created to make you feel strong emotions—often negative. These messages prey on and amplify the negative thought patterns we have developed through our own experiences and make us believe their propaganda.

We must find a way to be aware of what's going on in the world without falling into the abyss of the negativity that spurs hate and intolerance. Words and images are used to intensify our sense of fear. In the decade beginning in 2020, the challenges presented were unexpected and polarizing.

Absent these messages, we have our individual triggers making us feel disempowered. An interaction with a spouse may bring us back to a feeling we had as a child. The bosses' words tap into our deepest insecurities. Our amygdala is activated, and we are compelled to respond. Byron Katie, author, coach, and teacher, says, "The first act of war is a defense." There is no war and no battle if we don't react to the triggers around us. By creating awareness, we can stop the pattern of reacting to every trigger that pops up.

As you achieve greater awareness, you will be less reactive to situations and people. Reactions will never completely go away; you are only human, after all. But you will be better able to use your logical mind to evaluate, disregard, or solve issues in the moment. You will improve your skills as an observer, witnessing the complexities of situations. You will develop increased compassion for others, considering their own complex map of the world as you understand yours more deeply. This is a more effective way of learning from others. Increased awareness and understanding can only serve to bring more peace to a world that is often divided.

Sad and frustrating things happen in this world. Our goal is not to achieve a state that is devoid of emotion. We are looking to achieve perspective. You will be able to reserve your strong emotional reaction for when it's warranted and when it spurs actions of advocacy for those who need your voice, help, and support most. You'll be able to reduce the occurrences where your strong emotional reaction is wasted (such as social media debates). These types of interactions are not worthy of your energy. Having extreme emotions from everyday interactions and activities takes too much of your vital energy. This is energy that is best directed toward activities that will serve you and others.

Mindfulness

We want to visit the state of mindfulness as often as we can. Mindfulness is simply the act of witnessing and being deeply aware of what we're feeling and sensing. It is a place of non-judgment with limited or no interpretation. In the bustle of the day, we are running places, planning, and doing too many things. Obligations are stacked on a moving conveyer belt. This constant activity produces anxiety and stress and can lead to overwhelm and depression. These activities drain us of our energy, but through the practice of mindfulness, we're able to get back to a place of calm and peace.

An integral part of meditation is focusing on the breath. This is a mindfulness technique by itself. At any point in time, when you're feeling stressed, or you're having an overwhelming sense of anxiety, you can take a pause and focus on your breath. According to a 2013 Huffington Post article, *How Changing Your Breathing Can Change Your Life*, by Carolyn Gregoire, the simple act of focusing on your breath has several positive effects. These benefits include stimulating brain growth and development, improving heart rate variability, reducing stress and anxiety, and lowering blood pressure.

There are endless ways you can incorporate mindfulness into your daily life. Meditation, breathwork, and journaling have all been part of your transformational journey so far. Mindfulness requires that we stop the endless treadmill of activity. Slowing down and reducing frenetic activity is vitally important to get to a mindful state. Similarly, intently focusing on a mindful activity promotes a meditative response. Here are some other ways that you can jump-start your awareness and mindfulness.

· Take a bath. Use lavender and Epson salts to invoke feelings of calm.

· Get out in nature. Take a walk, and get a little vitamin D.

· Color. Remember how absorbed you used to get as a child, picking the right color and staying within the lines?

· Listen to music (music that doesn't trigger a negative memory and cause you to become overly emotional—whether angry or sad. No death-metal or sad love songs that remind you of a lost love).

· Dance like no one's watching.

· Create art—paint, photography, or any other form of art, including crafting.

· Practice gratitude. Shift your focus to what is going well instead of the negative.

· Gardening. Get your hands in some dirt and plant your favorite herbs, flowers, or plants.

As you perform these activities, make sure you take the time to bring your attention back to your thoughts as an impartial and curious observer. Practice coming back to the moment when your mind starts to wander. Let the worries of the past and the stress of the future just move past you as you enjoy the current moment.

Meditation

The practice of meditation has been an integral part of *The Nature of Transformation.* Simply put, meditation saved my life. Along my journey, I've come across those who state, "I just can't meditate." I have contemplated my stance on that statement for a long time: should everyone meditate? I try not to make sweeping assessments that *everyone* should do *anything*; however, I have come to believe that everyone really should meditate in some form. The world would be a better place if this were the case.

There is confusion about the purpose of meditation. Assumptions run the spectrum of it being a woo-woo spiritual practice to needing to clear your mind of all thoughts. The purpose of meditation is simply to be mindful. Removing all thoughts is not possible. Meditation is practicing non-judgmental awareness of your thought processes for a dedicated period. As thoughts come up, watch how they can easily pass without attaching to the thought. As you evolve your practice, at times (not every time), you'll be able to get to the perfect place of *now* where you're not stressing about the past or worrying about the future.

I try to meditate daily. It's my daily non-negotiable. Over time, I set up my altar with all my favorite things, including elements of the earth, essential oils, my favorite pillows, and blankets. My practice has evolved over time. I started my practice by listening to guided meditations. I have meditated alone and in group settings. I've alternated between music and silence. I've practice Kundalini mantra meditations. I have studied and meditated at my local Buddhist Temple. I've enjoyed sound healing/sound bath meditations in the middle of the California desert, at my local yoga studio and in a private session with a gifted sound healer. I studied and practiced Transcendental Meditation. There are endless methods and places to meditate. You just need to find the practice that works for you.

I have been solid in my practice for years now, and it has made me a calmer person. I am less reactive to negative situations and people. I would not be as far along in my personal healing without this practice. I have a greater sense of my personal self-worth. Starting my day with meditation as part of my morning routine, I have witnessed I am at my most creative and inspired self after my practice. I'm not weighed down by worrying about the day ahead of me.

Commit to daily meditation as part of your healing practice. No special equipment is required. Just a quiet space where you won't be interrupted. Start small and start easy. You don't need to sit in meditation for an hour every day. Five minutes consistently every day will pay significant dividends over time. Be patient with yourself because some sessions will feel incredible, and others will feel like they didn't work. Continue and evolve your practice based on your needs and desires.

3.3 Controlling the Inputs

I was 23, working in an office setting, and a coworker would start every morning with the bad news low-down. Starting with an account of the most horrific violent crimes, traffic accidents, neglected children, and people stealing and taking advantage of others. I didn't need to watch the news because every story was recounted with precise detail. It was a very harsh and heavy way to start the day. I would always ask her if there was any good news that day. Were there any good things happening in this world? Without knowing why, I instinctively began using this technique as mental health self-preservation.

Information is coming from every direction. Bad news and negativity make the best headlines, are the most salacious, and attract the biggest audience. We need to be discerning about what we let into our minds, how much and when. Negativity builds upon itself. If you are in a group of people who are complaining or have a pessimistic outlook, these attitudes tend to grow in volume and intensity among the group, changing your mood for the negative.

Just as negative energy multiplies, positive energy expands and multiplies. You need to guard your inputs like a soldier protecting their camp. If you find yourself around someone who is oozing negative energy and seems compelled to bring you down to their level, take control and steer the conversation away from the negativity. Chances are this will not work very well because they are so invested in their belief that the world is a cold, dark, and ugly place. Your only other option is to remove yourself from the situation. Get some distance. It is not your job to change their thinking.

I will offer this caveat, however. Life happens, and sometimes people need your grace and understanding, not platitudes about thinking positively or changing the topic to a more uplifting subject. If someone is going through a particularly difficult time in their life, such as a divorce, an illness, a death, or another significant life event, show them compassion. Offer the gift of time. Just be with them, watch a movie, get massages or pedicures. Get coffee, have a good meal, or go for a walk. Support them with things like errands, shopping, or childcare. Laugh or cry with them. Be patient, compassionate and loving. There are no right actions or words to say to make someone else feel better during these times. A good friend can sit with you through the discomfort, and that is all that is needed or required.

Self-confidence and self-esteem

Self-confidence is your external representation of your self-esteem. We can be our own worst enemies by setting expectations for ourselves that are unrealistic. When we don't measure up to our own expectations, our self-confidence and self-esteem take a hit.

The foundation of your self-confidence is your level of self-esteem. Self-esteem represents your internal feelings of worthiness. It reflects your reputation with yourself. Therefore, to increase your ability to go out and be confident in this world, your foundation of self-esteem should be solid.

You are worthy of doing amazing things in this world. It is your birthright, regardless of the circumstances that may have chipped away at your feelings of self-worth. Being on this earth makes you worthy. This concept I struggled with for a while. Being left alone for much of my early childhood naturally turned into deep feelings of being unworthy. The universal truth is that all humans are equally worthy, including me. It is something I need to remind myself of frequently.

Here are some truths about self-esteem:

· Being confident does not mean that you are arrogant. Do not buy into the trap of believing misogynistic social cues and stigmas. Strong women are feared because they can and have changed antiquated norms of society. Do not be afraid of your own strength and ambition. The bigger question is, are you having trouble stepping into your own power and owning your strength? Are you playing small to make others feel better or because you, yourself, do not feel worthy?

· If you are treating people respectfully and honoring others' opinions, then you need to ask yourself why your treatment of yourself is not consistent with your treatment of others. When your inner dialogue is telling you lies about your self-worth, you are treating yourself disrespectfully. Your negative self-talk is likely informed by an experience that is not happening today.

· A consistent theme throughout the book has been to identify the source of your thought processes. Once you understand the source, you can challenge if these thoughts and behaviors are working for you now. Do you feel unworthy due to a childhood experience? Are your feelings about yourself informed by a scared and lonely seven-year-old? Do those same conditions exist in your current situation? When you can identify the source and challenge the assumption of your negative thoughts, then you are able to release the power and control those thoughts have over you.

· Do not tie your self-esteem to a particular outcome or achievement. This is faulty ground on which to place your self-esteem. Your sense of self needs to be intact regardless of what happens externally. You can be disappointed by not getting the expected results; however, your high self-esteem will allow you to pivot and try again.

· Do you have an unreasonable expectation of perfection? Falling short of flawless may impact your self-esteem if you have unrealistic expectations of yourself. This is faulty thinking that "proves" your negative self-image true. Magic happens when people are true, authentic, and vulnerable.

· Are you trying something new? If you have ventured away from your comfort zone, your self-confidence may not be high, but your self-esteem should remain consistent. Just keep plugging along. Get some wins under your belt.

· Celebrate your successes, your unique skills, and strengths. Review the list of skills and strengths you created. Really think about all that you have accomplished. Add to the list. If you are over the age of 18, you have survived and thrived in the face of significant challenges and heartbreak.

· Poor self-esteem could manifest in being critical and judgmental of others. It can make us feel better about ourselves when we think others may be doing worse (in our perception). This is faulty ground to lay your self-esteem upon. To break this cycle, surround yourself with positive people and make extraordinary efforts to be kind to others. When you can be kind to others, you increase your ability to also be kinder to yourself. Remember, self-esteem is defined as your reputation with yourself. Therefore, you will never feel confident and self-assured if you are overly critical of others.

· Have you ever received a compliment and then provided the person complimenting you with a list of reasons why you were undeserving of the compliment? "Oh, it was nothing." "It didn't take that much work." "Anyone could have done it." Stop qualifying the compliments you receive. Accept praise with a simple thank you. Then really accept the praise in your heart. If you are around people who also deflect praise, gently bring them back to the moment and let them know how you genuinely appreciate them.

· Dr. Pat Allen has said, "Women need to feel good to do good; men need to do good to feel good." Women, you need to start feeling good—through radical self-care and wellness. Take care of your physical, emotional, mental, and spiritual wellbeing. Start doing things that make you feel good and start to eliminate the things in your life that make you feel bad.

TIME WITH THE COACH:

Complete the following questions and exercises to feed and nurture a powerful mindset.

· A negative thought I have about myself is:

· These statements are false because:

· The positive thought I can replace it with is:

Answer the following:

· What mindfulness techniques can you incorporate into your life? When will you start these activities?

· What current negative influences in your life contribute to negative thoughts or emotions?

· What strategies can implement to reduce or eliminate these influences?

· Create a list of the things you have done or accomplished of which you are most proud.

· How will you incorporate positive and uplifting messages into your daily life?

YOUR POWERFUL THINKING MEDITATION

ESSENTIAL OILS

The following essential oils are associated with mental clarity and strength. Basil strengthens the senses, cedarwood will offset negative thinking, lemongrass stimulates the mind, rose helps clear stale energy, and rosemary helps build confidence.

YOUR POWERFUL THINKING MANTRA

I choose the thoughts I think. I am empowered through positive thinking

YOUR POWERFUL THINKING BREATHING TECHNIQUE

Use the box breath breathing technique to calm the nervous system. Returning to a place of calm will enable you to increase your awareness and choose more powerful thinking.

Sit tall and take 2-3 deep cleansing breaths through your nose, expanding your belly and fully expelling the air on each out-breath.

Inhale to the count of 4. Pause for a count of four. Exhale to the count of four. Pause for a count of four. Repeat the cycle ten times before beginning the meditation below

YOUR POWERFUL THINKING MEDITATION

Find a comfortable sitting position. Sit up with a straight spine.

Do a body scan (see Honor Your Story Meditation)

Powerful thinking is always available to me. It is simple to increase my power every day.

Powerful thinking is being curious. I'm curious about myself and the world around me.

Being compassionate and showing compassion are powerful. I prioritize compassion for myself. By showing myself compassion, my compassion for others increases

Being aware of my thoughts is powerful. I practice awareness every day

I'm able to make decisions in my own best interest. The decisions I make are beneficial to my higher being

I demonstrate my power by being honest. I present my full self in an honest way

My power is expressed in my willingness to be an active participant in my own life and in my own well-being.

I show my power by being creative. Creativity gives me power because I'm able to develop new ideas to serve myself and others

As you come back to room awareness, slowly begin to open your eyes. Give yourself a moment.

Take the time to write any notes about what thoughts or feelings may have come up during your meditation

A WALK-THROUGH NATURE

THE RESTORATIVE OCEAN

The ocean simultaneously heals and frightens me. The immense power of the ocean somehow works together with its grounding force. The ocean is like life, complex and forever changing. It is life-giving and yet can sometimes feel like it's trying to consume you. The ocean does not take you into consideration. You have no ability to alter her. She will do what she wants to do when she wants to do it. She's relentless in pursuing her objectives. Along with her partner, the moon, she's the ultimate force of nature.

Spending most of my life in Southern California, I've had easy access to experience the ocean. As a kid, whenever one of my sisters wanted to go to the beach (to lay out on the sand, not go in the water), I would always go along. On the drive down, there would be a palpable shift in the temperature and composition of the air. Then the salt air would rush in. The distinct smell eased my anticipation, letting me know how close we were.

Staking our claim with our beach towels, I would venture down to the water by myself to dip my toes in the water. Slowly going in deeper until I was jumping over small waves. It was meditative before I knew what mediation was. In a chaotic childhood, the ocean represented that calmness that my soul needed. I thought perhaps the answers to the questions I had not even formed yet, existed in its vastness.

As an adult, when I needed to escape the chaos that still existed in my life, I drove down to the beach by myself. I felt the shift in my being as I started to smell the salty air. On those days I would sit near the shore, watching the rhythm of the waves. I would deepen my breathing in time with the waves.

The endless horizon promises that somewhere, somehow, there were answers out there. When your eyes cannot see beyond the ocean, you intellectually know that beyond the horizon, there is land. That's how I internalized the solutions to my problems. I could not see the answers, but I knew for sure that the answers were out there.

And now, I'm still pointed with great regularity to the ocean. In my meditation practice, I use angel oracles. "The Ocean" is one of the few cards that is presented to me time and again. The angels, my intuition or my spirit guides know exactly when I need the healing of water. The ocean gives me life, tranquility, and a connection to my spiritual side that I need to tap into.

The ocean can represent so many things. It offers a healing womb and signifies abundance in its endlessness. It reminds us of all the power that exists, not only in nature but within ourselves. It signifies the mysteries and the natural rhythms of life. It reminds us that there are some things so powerful that to try to control it would be futile. Finally, it brings a profound sense of calm and grounding.

Are you similarly drawn to the ocean? Maybe you're drawn to the night sky or the majesty of mountains. Think about a vast natural occurrence you feel particularly drawn to. How does it make you feel? Detail your experiences with these places. Honor the gifts that Mother Nature gives to us by simply enjoying these places and giving thanks.

SECTION

Fall – Harvest,
Transform, Preserve

Fall – Harvest, Transform, Preserve

F ALL IS THE TIME for the most significant changes and shifts to occur. Things start to slow down after a long hot summer. The days begin to get shorter, and the nights get longer. The moon is brighter, and the stars are more visible. This is the time to connect more deeply to your spirit. It's the time to give thanks and celebrate the bounty of your life.

4.1 Connect to Your Spirit

Your spirit is your life force. It is the vitality that you receive from having a deep connection to yourself and to a deeper understanding of life. It doesn't rely on material things or outside forces. It is always within you and longing for the truest, most joyful expression of your being. You don't need to be anyone other than who you are. You do not need to achieve anything. There is no need to earn anything or prove your worthiness. It's the part of you that longs for deeper meaning. It's the part of you that chose this book because, deep down, you know that you were meant for more happiness and fulfillment. It is the part of you that creates and is creative. It desires connection and healing.

Your spirit, in its purest form, expresses compassion, truth, and courage. Prioritize these attributes for yourself because when you can truly show compassion, truth, and courage for yourself, you're able to multiply these traits and send them out to the world.

Your spirit reflects your true nature and authentic self. Whether you realize it or not, this is what you long for. When you're feeling that ache that something may be missing from your life and you feel an emptiness, often the solution is to reconnect with the spiritual side of your being.

The most impactful way to honor your spirit is to fully commit to your healing journey. Eradicating all the muck that you've accumulated through your life's experiences that no longer serve your highest good will allow you to most effectively care for your spirit. Deep hurt and resentments act as barriers to your soul's freedom.

4.2 Resiliency Formula: Forgiveness, Acceptance, and Service

When you're caught in a cycle of anger and resentment, you will find it extremely hard to live the life you desire. I know this firsthand. Throughout my 20s and 30s, I was a terribly angry person. I carried a lot of resentment towards myself, my parents, my family, and my husband. It was slowing eating away at me like a cancer. There have been pivotal times in my life when I realized the circumstances I was living were changing the person I was at my core. My anger was turning me into someone I didn't like.

I was able to experience brief moments of lightness but was still mostly enveloped by a dark and stormy sky. Seeing those flickers of light, I realized that I must do something differently. I was afraid if I didn't take control of my own healing and harness the light, I could very well be trapped by my own bitter darkness.

Forgiveness can be complicated. Often forgiveness is inaccurately equated to absolving people of taking responsibility for their bad behavior. The people who hurt you may not even be asking you for your forgiveness. Perhaps, like me, you've been embattled with people with narcissistic traits who may never acknowledge the impact their behaviors have had on you. In fact, they may not even be deserving of your compassion or kindness. There's a famous, unattributed quote that says, "An apology without change is manipulation." That act of forgiveness should never be confused with allowing yourself to be continually re-victimized by someone else's bad behavior.

I had a lot of anger toward my mom. I wanted to forgive her but knew there would be no conversation where the two of us worked work to create a resolution. It just wasn't in her. Even though I would never get that ideal reconciliation moment, I knew that I wanted and needed to forgive her. If

I didn't, I would not have been able to let go of the anger I held inside.

When you no longer have a sparring partner, anger and sadness only have one place to reside—within you. My reason for forgiving was my own psychological survival. There was never to be a movie-like ending where I was able to express my sadness, disappointment, or anger. And she would say something loving and magical, and there would be closure. Pan out and roll the credits as we share a teary-eyed embrace.

The two questions that started me on the road to forgiveness were, "What if she was doing the best she could at the time?" and "What must have done to her for her to have done this to me?" Whether you get the answers to those questions or not (I never did), the result is an understanding that the behavior I experienced wasn't *about* me.

There is a wide range of damage humans inflict on one another. Most detrimental behavior is a cycle of repeated trauma or mental illness passed down. It doesn't make it right, and it doesn't excuse it. The objective is to stop the cycle of inflicting pain on ourselves and onto others around us. The act of forgiveness removes the responsibility and burden from your shoulders that you did something to deserve it.

Realizing that the neglect I experienced wasn't a result of my being unlovable or unworthy has been vital in my process of healing and forgiveness. The journey starts with first showing compassion to yourself.

Forgiveness is not letting the other person off the hook for what they've done. It's a spiritual journey to eradicate the destruction and damage that was done to your soul. It's a journey to try to understand, to the best of our ability, where the lessons are and perhaps where humanity and compassion reside. It's the process by which you start to slowly let go of the anger that is only negatively impacting your life now.

The act of forgiving doesn't need to be done with the person you're holding anger for. I didn't forgive my mother in person. I didn't need her to receive my forgiveness to be able to forgive her. I forgave her years before she died. When she did die, I didn't have any anger in my heart. I wasn't holding onto any unresolved feelings. Given the complexity of the relationship, I was curious if I would have any regrets when she passed. The relationship certainly wasn't ideal, but it felt resolved. Nothing felt unfinished, and I don't carry around that hurt. It feels good not to carry that weight around.

If you find the act of forgiveness difficult, that's ok. Everyone has their own healing process. You may never get to the place of full forgiveness. It does not mean that you cannot heal. Consider invoking the act of acceptance instead. Accept and honor your experiences. Wishing for a different outcome is tortuous. No matter how hard I wished for a nurturing mother, it would never be true.

Accept that you are worthy of living a good and happy life. Acceptance means that you know deep in your heart that if someone caused you trauma in your life, it is not because of you. You did not cause their bad behavior. They reenacted their experienced trauma onto you. You were the recipient of someone's hurtful actions. Not the cause of someone's hurtful actions. These traumatic events all too often cause us to believe that we are deserving of this behavior or are unlovable and unworthy. This is just not the case.

Nobel Peace Prize Laureate Aung San Suu Kyi said, "When you're feeling helpless, help somebody." The final component of the Resiliency Formula is service. You had these experiences. There is no changing that fact. In some cases, these experiences have changed the person you are. The most powerful thing you can do when you're feeling helpless is helping someone else. Turn your gifts, your knowledge, and your passion back out into the world and help others. When you help others, you heal yourself. This is what I've done through my coaching and writing is to my share my healing journey so I can inspire and teach others to do the same. I have an opportunity to take the skills I've gained during my healing journey, my training, and education to try to serve others.

If there is the potential to truly heal a relationship with someone where you are not righteous in your anger, the other person is open to your perspective, and you're open to theirs, you should absolutely try. When two people can truly connect on a level of compassion and understanding, there is no better medicine for your soul.

You were *meant* to survive and thrive in the face of this adversity that was handed to you. You did nothing to deserve this hardship. This experience is intended for your spiritual growth.

Forgiveness Breathwork

· Breath in for a count of four; hold for a count of four; release for a count of four (4:4:4).

· Do this breath five times.

· On the sixth time, breathe in and remember the encounter you are trying to forgive someone for. Breathe out.

· Continued focused breathing while you relive the memory in your head. Focus on the feelings you're having as that moment replays in your mind.

· Pause the memory. Do two 4:4:4 breaths. Focus just on your breathing. Feel the breath enter your body, feel the breath suspended in your body and feel the full release of the breath from your body.

· Continued with your focused breath and relive the memory again, but this time from the perspective of the other person. What feelings are you having as them during this remembered encounter?

· Do two more 4:4:4 breaths.

· Take one final deep breath in. Hold for a count of ten. As you fully release the breath, forgive the other person, and forgive yourself.

4.3 Gratitude

> "The real voyage of discovery consists not in
> seeking new landscapes,
> but in having new eyes."
> —Marcel Proust

The proximity of living a grateful existence is adjacent to living a content and happy life. Gratitude is a necessity, like the air we breathe. It's the gateway action and emotion to feeling good. Sanity and peace will have a hard time existing in your life for any sustained period without feeling gratitude. Gratitude is feeling all the good feelings now, not contingent on being able to achieve the next thing. Those feelings of satisfaction and pride are available to you now. A life filled with all striving and wanting creates a life of comparison, feelings of inferiority, wanting more, and never feeling satisfied.

I believe in always having a goal for your life because I believe in continuous growth and learning. The things that I want to achieve are not because I'm trying to fill a hole but because I want to see what I'm truly capable of. I want to try new things. I want to create a positive impact on the world. I want to spend my days doing things that bring me as much joy as possible.

Achievement, for achievement's sake, provides only short-term satisfaction. When you have a strong desire for something and achieve your goals, the positive feelings are fleeting. The feeling is not the result of finally having the thing you worked and waited for. Material things, money, achievements, or advancement won't fill the hole you're trying to fill.

This is where the practice of gratitude fits in. Gratitude is the appreciation for the wisdom and lessons you learned along the way. It's being thankful for how the experience enriched you and brought you joy. It's satisfaction in the knowledge that you were able to persevere through adversity. It's the pride you feel in yourself. It's not the new car in the driveway. It's not the thing. It's never the thing. It's always the feeling. And those feelings are available to you without the achievement.

Gratitude is easy when life is easy. Gratitude is hardest when one is in the midst of a difficult season. When I've been most challenged and struggle to get out of bed, I turn to gratitude. A gratitude practice during these times is not a magic pill. It does not put a bounce back in my step; I'm not immediately whistling and skipping around. What it does is get my feet on the floor. It grounds me in my purpose. It presents me with the possibility that there may be an opportunity to learn and grow from the challenges I am facing at that moment. It creates physical movement that benefits the mind, body, and spirit.

Gratitude also possesses magical qualities. With the practice of gratitude, the negative emotions that bring so much toxicity into our lives start to wane. We begin to lose feelings that leave us with an ache in our hearts, like envy, regret, resentment, and jealousy.

It is only logical, then, that you cannot be in a state of gratitude and feel jealous in the same moment. The two emotions are not harmonious. One will prevail. Wouldn't you rather the winner be an emotion that makes you feel good rather than one that makes you feel horrible?

Another side effect is less stress. Probably the most stress I've felt to date is a result of my corporate jobs. Corporate America doesn't own the right to stressful working conditions. The experience of restructuring, re-organizations, lay-offs and just a large amount of people with really strong personalities vying for position and attention creates a level of stress that can really take a toll on your wellbeing. If you work at anything for 8-10 hours a day for five days a week, hustling to earn a paycheck, you know what stress feels like. Gratitude for the life that this job has afforded you, the people you've met, and the extensive learning and growth you have no doubt earned will help you effectively manage the stress levels of the capital grind most of us must endure.

There are some practical ways to put a gratitude practice in place to improve the quality of your life

· Using any planner or journal where you can easily list at least three things that you are grateful for every day. The practice of physically writing words down is therapeutic. It stimulates brain cells and improves your memory. By writing down what you are grateful for, you are imbedding these thoughts and ideas into your psyche. Be detailed and specific in your daily gratitude. Include the reason why you are grateful for the items on your list.

- When life gets murky, start with the smallest of things. A warm cup of coffee, sunshine or rain, a place to lay your head at night.

- The fastest way to appreciate what you have is to help those who have less than you do. If you are in a cycle of feeling down and you have the means, find a cause near and dear to your heart, and support those less fortunate.

- Make a list of what you are good at, what you know how to do, and the places you feel most confident. Focus your attention on doing these activities, and really appreciate the unique skills you have and the pleasure you derive from doing them.

- Check yourself for feelings of entitlement. Entitlement is a killer of gratitude. No one is more deserving than another person.

- Are you too focused on a particular outcome? Remember, you are after the feelings of peace and happiness. Placing your happiness all in one basket where the achievement of something determines whether you feel good or not is risky. Your happiness should not be contingent upon a particular outcome.

- Are you in a cycle of comparison? Coveting what other people have will never lead to feelings of contentment, happiness, or gratitude.

- Do you foster an understanding that all situations are impermanent? If you are having a difficult season, understand that "this too shall pass" will help you gain perspective.

My mantra during these times is, "this is just a moment in time."

· Is your thinking inflexible? Do you live in a black and white world with little variation of color? When you can see multiple sides of complex situations and your thinking is adaptable, you will have a better probability of being able to sit in gratitude.

· Is your focus on your dreams, or is it focused on your disappointments? How much space does regret take up in your brain? Regret is meant to be a temporary emotion that drives you to modify your approach going forward. Maya Angelou said, "When you know better, you do better." This concept is the antidote to regret.

· Vocalize your gratitude. Tell those around you how grateful you are for them and why. You will compound the effect by making others feel good as well.

4.4 Passionate Living. Find inspiration. Discover your passion. Live with purpose.

As the pandemic started and quarantine went from 3 weeks to multiple months, I realized I was getting further and further away from being inspired and working on the things I was passionate about. Most days felt like a chore. It was hard to be joyful. This pandemic brought an amplified desire in me to hunker down. My introverted self welcomed shelter-in-place with open arms and strategized to make it a permanent lifestyle choice. My reaction to stress and anxiety is to get very still and make no sudden movements.

If I'm honest with myself, I've been in the midst of this struggle for two years prior to the pandemic beginning. I was in an unhealthy work situation that ripped and tore at my confidence. I stopped doing the things I loved while endlessly trying to fit a square peg into a round hole. I focused all my energy on fixing the unfixable. I ended up depleted by the hopelessness of it all.

2020 continued to serve one hit after another: a friend's illness and passing at a young age, a back injury, home remodeling challenges, social injustice, and a draining political environment.

I lost my passion. I had no inspiration. I was in survival mode. Sometimes you just need to survive and focus your attention on extricating yourself from situations that aren't healthy while using the time to reset and heal your heart (and your body).

As I started to emerge from the funk that was 2020, my existential crisis arrived just in time. I realized I was paying a high price for not living passionately and not doing the things that brought me joy. I wasn't doing what I was called to do, what I'm passionate about. I wasn't feeling passionate about anything anymore because too much time had passed since I immersed myself in those activities. I felt an overwhelming dullness to life and an ache that kept whispering to me, "Get back to doing what you love."

But first, I needed to find inspiration. I dedicated time to getting my hands in some dirt by planting flowers and herbs. Meticulously placing tiny seeds in the dirt. Hoping to see life emerge in two weeks. You might think this ambitious project to have fresh herbs in my summer salads means that I have a green thumb. The opposite is true. In fact, those who truly know me likely call me a plant serial killer behind my back.

But I keep trying to make things grow. I keep buying plants even though there is a dismal and historic (and generous) 25% survival rate. I keep trying because I love the feeling of getting lost in the act of planting, daily watering, and (hopefully) watching growth and transformation. This miracle of nature inspires me.

Through doing inspirational activities, I started to find the energy I need to do what I'm passionate about again. It can be tough to get motivated to reignite your passion after a break (or in my case, a breakdown). But it's so important to rebound back to the state of creativity and motivation. There's a high cost to pay when you suspend passionate living.

If you've put passionate living on hold, here are some of the costs you may be incurring and signs you need to start to ignite your passions.

· Your dreams become farther and farther away from reality. Do you even remember what they are?

· You find no joy in the work that you're doing. Life is mundane and repetitive.

- You have no energy or motivation.

- You're beginning to let other people define your path and defer to what *they* think you should be doing.

- You keep postponing things until "tomorrow," but tomorrow never arrives.

- Your thoughts about life are either "Is that all there is?" or "It's good enough."

- Your productivity levels have dipped, and you're disorganized and less efficient.

- You call in sick, or your performance on the job is suffering.

- Alternatively, you are a workaholic and find you have no energy left to dedicate to things you genuinely enjoy.

Nine Truths About Passionate Living

1. **You Are Meant to Live a Joyful and Passionate Life.**

Life is not meant to be hard. Life *is* hard because, well, it's life. The glorious space between the hard times is intended to be lived with joy and passion. I know this for sure. You are meant to bring this elevated, high-vibration self to this world for a purpose. Your light shines so others can see through their own darkness. Your light makes people realize that they also have the light within themselves. Don't deny yourself, and do not deny others of this light.

Give yourself permission to live passionately.

2. **Passionate Living isn't Contingent Upon Achievements or Other People.**

Don't live in the "when" cycle. When I get the money, when I have the time, when I'm the perfect size, when I meet the perfect person, then I will live passionately. The problem with contingencies is there is no guarantee of any of these things showing up. So, you wait for the perfect time. And you wait. And you wait.

Placing your passion in the hands of contingencies is a dangerous habit. It's a faulty ground where your dreams are more likely to fall through the cracks. Your passions exist within you already. *Now* is the perfect time to begin.

Start slow and be kind to yourself. Dedicate and schedule small amounts of time, daily or even weekly, to spend on a passion project. This is not wasted time.

Stop waiting to live passionately.

3. **Recognize the Role of Passion in Your Purpose.**

If passion is what your soul is calling you to do, and it's the thing you can lose yourself in doing, then your purpose is who you become by living a passionate life. You cannot realize the full extent of who you are and your purpose here on this earth without stepping into your passions. The foundation of your purpose is to live the most joyful, healthy, and full existence in this lifetime that you've been gifted. This full person can then manifest their purpose. Without passion, purpose doesn't show up.

When you marry your passion and your purpose, you bring to light those unique skills and talents you possess. The essence of your being intersects with your personality to bring an elevated self to the forefront.

Living passionately is an essential component of living a purposeful life.

4. **The Universe Will Step In and Take Charge if You Don't.**

The universe has a tricky way of working. She will give you reminders, clues, and opportunities. She will nudge you in the direction of your passion. If you ignore the signs, she will become slightly more aggressive—in your best interest, of course. You can resist her guidance. You always have free will. But she won't forget, and she will never give up on you. Lean into her guidance. She will hold you up when you feel like falling back. You can trust that she won't let you fail. You can trust that she has knowledge of your capabilities and believes you are gifted beyond your imagination. She's invested in you and making your dreams come true.

Notice the signs the universe provides.

5. **Listen to the Whispers**

Do you ever find yourself doing regular daily tasks, then the thought pops into your head, "You should—" Mine are always, "You should write," and "You're a writer." It also whispers for me to do all sorts of creative things like paint, go out in nature, garden, take pictures. The whispers I'm talking about are the kind, loving whispers, not the hateful ones. The kind ones are telling you the truth. The hateful, negative whispers are *liars*, and the source is fear. The kind whispers know what's in your heart.

We hear the whispers, then we question and doubt them. People who get the loving whisper to write then try to argue with it, "But I'm not a writer" (hateful whisper). If you get the whisper, "You're a writer," you *are* indeed a writer. Because people who are not writers don't get the whisper to write. They get another whisper. They get the whisper to apply for that promotion. Their whisper tells them to talk to that person and take that course that leads them down a certain path. They get the whisper to take that trip, go to that retreat, and pick up a paint brush.

The other whispers I get to paint, spend time in nature, and take pictures, are supportive whispers. They are the whispers that tell me to go out and get inspired. Get your creative juices flowing. The whisper doesn't tell me I *am* a painter or photographer. It *does* tell me I'm a writer.

Get still and trust the whispers.

6. Don't Forget the Inspiration

My passion is not nature photography. Nature photography is my inspiration. Inspiring activities are like fertilizer to your passions. You need to feed your passions with activities that inspire you. Planting an herb garden is not my passion. But the act of gardening and watching things grow stimulates my mind.

My passions are helping people through coaching and writing. I have had a lot of fear around putting myself out there, taking a chance on myself, and facing criticism. Therefore, inspiration is so critical. When you get lost in creativity, your mind starts to open. It becomes receptive to dreaming and imagining what could be. You start to release the negativity and doubt. This also happens during exercise and walks in nature, hanging out at the beach, and sticking your feet in the water. These are life-giving activities that are meant to spur your passions. Don't skip the inspiration.

If you find yourself unsure about what you're passionate about doing, accelerate your inspiration, and it will materialize.

7. **Passions are Mutable**

We put so much pressure on ourselves to find our passions and our purpose. "Is it the right one? How will I know? What if I lose passion for what I choose? I don't have just one. Which one do I choose?"

Very few people come out of the womb knowing that they have the skills and desire to be a concert pianist or some other outwardly obvious gift. For most of us, it takes time and reflection to determine what we are passionate about.

Choosing a passion is not a life sentence. It's not a contract written in blood. As we evolve, so do our interests and our passions. As we learn and grow, our passions align with our new knowledge about ourselves and life in general.

It's okay to have multiple passions, and it's okay for your passions to change over time. It is also perfectly okay to not know what your passion is. This is your free ticket to explore. Your passion can be found when you're feeling the most joy. Just like true love, it will show up when you're not looking.

Don't hold on too tight. Release expectations (internal and external) and focus instead on finding inspiration.

8. Don't Get Addicted to Distractions

We get sucked into the drama and the *shoulds* of life. Then we acclimate to our busyness and stress. So, we delay our passions. We put them on the back burner and wait for the day when we can get back to doing the things we love. Our obligations become a reasonable and justifiable excuse to delay passionate living. No one can fault you for prioritizing children, parents, bills, or other life necessities. The longer we delay our passions, the more fear sets in. "But I'm not very good at it." "It won't turn out as I imagine." "People will judge me." "People will call me selfish." "I *am* selfish." (Remember the bad whispers—they lie). Eventually, we turn a temporary situation into a permanent excuse. Busy and stressed are excuses when it's really fear that's keeping you stuck.

You know you're in trouble when you start looking for the drama. Gossiping, picking fights, and obsessing over insignificant things, are all ways we choose drama over joy. Don't seek out distractions and become addicted to the temporary gratification it gives you by alleviating your fear of failure (or success).

Detox yourself from distractions by scheduling time every day to dedicate to your passions.

9. Don't Go Too Long Without Passionate Activity

There's danger in living without passion. Your life starts to dull. It begins to look black and white and gray. The edges soften, and the texture and the detail fade. Then apathy and boredom set in. You start to care less and less about the regular things going on around you. The only thing worse than apathy is depression. You may feel sad and even a bit lonely because it's like you lost a best friend. But what you really lost is yourself.

Don't forget what it feels like to live in your passion. Bath in it. Get lost in something before you completely lose your desire to do so.

Passionate living shouldn't be a chore. It's a gift. Everyone needs passion in their life. It is what makes us feel human and alive. My passion is to help others believe that they are worthy and deserving of living a passionate life and understand that a passionate life is self-less, not selfish. My passion is to deliver this message to you and hopefully inspire you to live your best life – the life you deserve to live. This world needs your most alive, most evolved, and joyful self. This is the way we transform ourselves and transform the world.

TIME WITH THE COACH

· What are you passionate about doing? Any answer is ok. Do not limit yourself. Don't think of all the reasons why it's crazy or unattainable. Having the answer "I don't know yet" is perfectly okay.

· What unique skills or abilities do you possess? Note: everyone has unique skills and abilities. Don't be shy. Don't be humble. List them *all*.

· What is preventing you from acting on your passions? List one way to overcome each barrier.

· What is your cost for not living passionately?

Which of the Nine Truths resonated with you the most and why?

1. You Are Meant to Live a Joyful and Passionate Life

2. Passionate Living Isn't Contingent Upon Achievements or People

3. Recognize the Role of Passion in Your Purpose

4. The Universe Will Step In and Take Charge if You Don't

5. Listen to the Whispers

6. Don't Forget Inspiration

7. Passions are Mutable

8. Don't Get Addicted to Distractions

9. Don't Go Too Long Without Passionate Activity

Make a list of the things that give you inspiration.

List 3 ways you can prioritize living or discovering your passion <u>today</u>.

Final words to set you on your path:

· If you are unable to articulate your passion, don't feel bad. Simply relax and do as many inspirational activities as you can.

· List your passion on a post-it and place it in a prominent place where you have a daily reminder to prioritize your passions.

4.5 Fostering Connection

> "A deep sense of love and belonging is an irreducible need of all people. We are biologically, cognitively, physically, and spiritually wired to love, to be loved, and to belong."—Brené Brown

Let's face it, we can't get through this life alone. We need to find our people. We need people, and people need us. We are born with the need to feel connected to others. We want a safe place to fall, people who know us—warts and all and still want to be around us. Having meaningful and positive relationships in our lives not only improves the quality of life, but studies have shown it also extends our lives. Having a diverse tribe of people who have similar interests, share some of your core beliefs, enjoy doing similar things, and who you can share your authentic self with is critical to our survival.

Your connections should include those family and friends who, even though you may not share the same interests, know, and respect you. You need people around you who respectfully challenge your way of thinking. You need to have people who raise the bar and who have high expectations of you.

My approach to developing and maintaining connections in my life is cautious and complicated. This is and will likely always be an area of my life that I need to make sure I maintain some balance. It is on my watch-list. My conditioning has been one of solitude. Solitude is easy. It aligns with my introversion, but it really goes deeper than that for me. For most of my childhood, I was alone, whether anyone was around me or not. I don't share my feelings easily. I've prioritized other people's feelings most of my life. In my perception, everyone else always had more, bigger, and more painful feelings that dwarfed mine. Hence, I began the habit of not expressing my feelings at all. That pattern has played out my whole life and continues to be an issue that I work to counteract. I find it incredibly hard to reach out to people and even harder to ask anyone for even the slightest bit of help or support. But deep down, I long for that connection. We all do.

I've trained myself over these many, many years to lean into the feelings of discomfort so that I can come out on the other side and find that connection with people. I maintain a small circle of friends. I continuously find my "people" through exploring groups and events, mostly in the wellness community. I have found people with like interests through studios and gyms, going to see authors or inspirational speakers at events and conferences. People have moved in and out of my life for various reasons. I don't fear this anymore because I have the knowledge that people are often in your life to teach you something about yourself, friendship, or human nature. Not all these relationships are lifelong connections.

When you have your "people" around you, you can share pieces of yourself, be vulnerable, and hold someone else's vulnerability with loving care. You develop a deeper sense of empathy and simply are a kinder person. Foster your connections and tend to relationships as you would a prized garden.

4.6 Energy Management

> "You are a latticework of energies."—Donna Eden, Energy Medicine

Your energy may be your greatest asset, or it may be the thing that keeps you separate and always longing. When I bought my first house, I was going through a separation. It was a scary time. The financial responsibility of owning a home was combined with the fear and heaviness of breaking up a family. I was angry and depressed. I was embarking on this home-buying journey alone. This is the sort of thing you usually do with a life partner. Although I was excited about the new home, my negative energy was palpable and oozed with fear and sadness. I thought I was keeping these feelings undercover. I grew up with the ability to suppress my feelings. I tried pushing my feelings down, as I had done all my life.

Sitting in the new home I purchased, I would stew in my feelings. My son, trying to enjoy his first non-rental family home, would bring friends over to swim in the pool. My son, sweet and intelligent, can dish out doses of truth in a succinct way that can bring me to my knees. He's not overly emotional or compassionate in his delivery, which can feel brutal. I was in a perpetual ugly emotional state when he told me that none of his friends liked to come over to the house because I looked so mean and angry all time. Gut punch.

I wish I could say that I was immediately able to come out of that space. I was making the biggest transition of my life, and I didn't feel positive and friendly. But his words stung me and stuck with me. This was when I began the difficult and focused work of personal healing, improving my life, and increasing my happiness.

Your energy is on display for others to see and feel. Whether you intend them to feel it or not. Emotions are contagious. People around you will start mirroring your energy, or you will mirror theirs. Your energy then impacts how you live your life. It impacts your ability to have dreams and aspirations and has a direct effect on your ability to achieve those ambitions.

Your feelings, thoughts, and intentions, whether they are conscious or unconscious, positive, or negative, will attract people and experiences into your life that reflect your own energy. The quality of your energy and your thoughts are connected to your ability to live the life that you want to live. The law of attraction is a universal truth. Everything we can see and everything we cannot see is composed of energy. Your thoughts create energy; therefore, wherever your thoughts are focused, energy flows in that direction. That is why the vibration of our thoughts and emotions is one of the most forceful powers we possess as human beings.

We need to cultivate an environment where positive thinking is the norm, not an anomaly. It takes practice, it takes making it a habit, and it takes tools to bring yourself back to that state when you stray. We all stray because we are spiritual beings living the human experience. Feeling the opposite of positive feelings helps us identify what we do and do not want in our lives. We will experience heartache and disappointment. There is no way around it. But these are not permanent states of being. We need to keep bringing ourselves back to thoughts that will compound positive energy.

4.7 Your Authentic Self; Self-love and Self-Acceptance

Every part of this workbook has been leading you up to this point. Finding your authentic self and being okay with who you are is critical to this work. You've already been doing the work - scrubbing off all the layers that have been built up around you to reemerge as your true self. Your acceptance and love of *you* are mandatory for your transformation.

Unlearning false beliefs that you or others have placed upon you and eliminating (or dramatically reducing) all the "shoulds" of who others think you should be, is a priority in all our healing journeys.

Sometimes we lose ourselves in the trauma of childhood, the demands of parenthood, or the quest to build a career and life for ourselves. You lose the quirky self, the dork within, or the brainiac trying to blend. Well, now it's time to reclaim all that you are and release everything you are not.

I've always had this internal push/pull feeling of trying not to stand out too much while also needing to be seen. We all want to be seen and appreciated for who we truly are, but that's a very vulnerable place to be—where you allow your authentic self to show through. You must love and appreciate who you are to be able to allow others to be able to see you for who you truly are. Having a fear of being your authentic self simply means that you are not loving yourself enough. A *Course in Miracles* states that we need to choose love over fear. Choose self-love instead of the fear of being seen for your authentic self.

Are you able to show up in this world with no mask? No hiding? Not trying to fit in or get along just for the sake of getting along? Are you comfortable in your own skin? Do you like you? Have you even gotten to know and accept the real you? Can you accept all your flaws and embrace all your gifts?

I remember in my 20s hearing the phrase, "You need to love yourself before you can truly love anyone else." I pushed the concept away. Self-love certainly wasn't accessible (or so I thought) to me in my 20s. It didn't seem realistic or practical. But now, so many years later, I realize it couldn't be truer. Without self-love and self-acceptance, how can you find someone to love you for who you truly are when *you* don't love who you truly are?

Self-love is an action. Just as you would foster a romantic relationship with actions to maintain that love and connection, the actions you take to show yourself appreciation compound and turn into a sense of love and confidence. Acts of self-love include:

1. Taking care of your physical health. It's so very hard to feel good and be authentic when you don't like the way you feel physically. Meet your physical needs through sleep, nutrition, and exercise. If this is an area of concern for you, go back and review that part of this book and make sure to put this area on your "watch-list."

2. Distancing yourself from people who do not honor your authentic self. If you spend a lot of time with people who criticize you and others, you will never feel like showing up authentically. Those people typically are very unhappy with themselves and project their self-judgment onto those around them. Find people who accept you just as you are.

3. Spending time alone. To be authentic, you need to be able to spend time with yourself. Going out to eat by yourself (honestly, this is still a challenge for me), going to a movie (this I love, no one to arrange schedules and seats with, no popcorn sharing issues). Travel and go on a vacation alone. Start with a long weekend. I've just started doing this. It's a little weird at first, but after the first day, it's freeing. There are countless things you can do. Start small if you're not used to being alone. If you always have significant other, a kid, a friend, or a colleague with you, start venturing off alone.

4. Trying new things. To be authentic to who you are, you need to test new possibilities and areas of interest. If you have always fancied being a photographer, but the extent of your capability is turning the camera on, take a class. Make a list of the things you would like to try. Set yourself a goal to try one new activity every month. You will not learn anything new about yourself when you keep doing the things you have always been good at.

5. Giving up shame. Shame shows up when you feel wrong or foolish as a character trait versus a behavior. It's the difference between I *am* selfish versus I *acted* selfishly. No one's perfect. We do things that we realize later that

there may have been a better approach. Shame is a killer of authenticity. Shame is a killer of all good feelings. You can't feel confident and shame. You can't feel creative and shame. You can't feel joy and shame. If this resonates with you, go read every Brené Brown book immediately.

6. Eradicating shame's cousin, guilt. You should not feel guilty about self-care, personal development, taking time for yourself, or having big dreams. Where is this guilt coming from? Are you placing undue pressure on yourself? Or is it someone else placing their expectations on you? This is *your* life. If someone serves you up a big dose of guilt, asking you to prioritize their thoughts and opinions about your life over your own, ask yourself, who's being selfish in that situation?

7. Knowing your deepest convictions and values. Know what you stand for and what is important to you. Understand your values and the things you will stand up for in life and apply these values to yourself. You must know your most basic expectations and what things are deal breakers in your life.

TIME WITH THE COACH:

Forgiveness

Who do you need to forgive and why?

What do you need to forgive yourself for?

How has anger or sadness from past events held you back?

What could you do in your life if you weren't holding onto anger?

If I were to forgive _____, it would mean_____.

Challenge the meaning of the above statement. Is it true?

If you feel that you cannot forgive at this time, what needs to happen for you to embark on a journey of forgiveness?

Is holding onto anger along with the physical and mental consequences sustainable?

Gratitude

What practices from the page in the gratitude section or other practices of your own can you start doing today?

Connection

Do you have enough satisfying supporting relationships in your life?

What's holding you back from making connections? What past experiences prevent you from letting people into your life?

Who are your most significant relationships with? Are they uplifting and mutually beneficial, negative, and unhealthy, or neither uplifting nor negative?

For those relationships that you would like to make changes to, what actions can you take?

Energy

Describe the energy you feel you put into the universe?

Ask a few people you're close with and trust what type of energy they get from you.

What energy do you *want* people to feel from you?

Self-acceptance

What are your top ten values in life?

YOUR SPIRIT MEDITATION

ESSENTIAL OILS

The following essential oils are associated with spiritual awakening. Cedarwood allows you to ground yourself in spirituality. Rosemary is effective for rituals and purification. Lavender has a grounding effect in mediation and prayer

YOUR SPIRIT MANTRA

I let my spirit soar through self-love, connection, appreciation, and authenticity

YOUR SPIRIT BREATHING TECHNIQUE

Conscious breathing. Breathe as you normally would. Don't alter your breath in any way. Observe the rhythm of your breath. Notice the changes in your breathing.

Watch how your breath enters your body
through your nose.

Notice how your chest and your belly expand as the air
enters your body.

Feel the air, the life force, in your lungs.

Release your breath.

Do this breathing in your own natural rhythm.

YOUR SPIRIT MEDITATION

Begin sitting in a comfortable position, spine straight, the top of your head reaching towards the sky.

For a few minutes, practice conscious breathing.

In the rhythm of your breath, breathe in and say:
I am pure energy.

As you breathe out, say: I let my spirit soar.

Keep breathing and keep repeating the phrase.

If your mind wanders, as it naturally will, simply return to the phrase and observe your breath.

When you're ready to come back to awareness, slowly and gently open your eyes.

Give yourself a moment.

Take the time to write any notes about what thoughts or feelings may have come up during your meditation

A WALK-THROUGH NATURE

RED REEF CANYON'S SANCTUARY

The Red Reef Canyon Trail was one of the many destinations planned for our weeklong visit to the national parks and trails in Utah during a family trip. It was July, and temperatures were hovering around a hundred degrees. When my son and I arrived at the trail at 11:00 a.m., the sun and the heat were blazing. I felt the heat radiating from above but also reflecting upwards from the ground, engulfing us.

With my camera, plenty of water, and my energetic son in the lead, I set out on the trail. The heat kept other explorers away. We saw a few disappointed swimmers exiting the trail when they realized the pools of water normally trapped in the slick rock bowls were all but dry.

We persevered through the trail surrounded by the towering red rocks, which during the sun's proudest moment in the middle of the day, did not provide much shade or relief from the heat.

I was determined to keep up with my son, willing my tired muscles to continue past the enormous fallen and aged tree trunks, prickly bushes, and sandy trails. My inner voice was telling me that I should turn around and go back to the comfort of the air-conditioned car. My inner critic was berating me for not being fit enough or young enough to bounce up the trail. But my son's youthful exuberance and my curiosity (along with plenty of water breaks under a few shaded areas) spurred me on.

We turned a corner and entered a shaded cove. This place was nothing short of an extraordinary private oasis. Outside of the summer months, as online pictures showed, this place is usually full of water from Quail Creek. On this mid-summer day, it contained small puddles of the aquatic ecosystem remnants hoping to survive the summer season.

Beyond this place is a more challenging trail. My son explored past the oasis, but I knew my limits and hanging by a rope off a one-hundred-foot ledge exceeded them. I found a spot and rested in the life-giving shade while also finding interesting areas to photograph.

Unexpectedly, the oasis started to whir with a dozen dragonflies darting in and around me. I tried to capture them with my camera set on a fast-action setting, but I was no match for their speed and playfulness. My desire to photograph the things around me often competes with the desire to simply experience what's happening. The Universe was telling me to "just be still." In my stillness, I was able to sit, breathe and take it all in. I didn't need to do or accomplish anything in this moment. It was an invitation to slow down and recognize the strength I had along the long and arduous journey to get there. In the stillness, I was able to recognize that although there was a struggle to get there, the oasis and miracles in the form of these dragonflies appeared. I was able to push myself gently through the obstacles and realize that this moment and this oasis were created just for me.

The dragonfly symbolizes change and transformation. They urge us to experience the moment and recognize the joy that is in the present. The presence of an oasis in the desert is where life is sustained, providing shelter. It also symbolizes where God or the Divine can be found. Glory and grace are the gifts of an oasis.

The powerful messages nature provides each time you commune with her are significant and powerful. My message that day and the message that I've carried with me from that magical experience is one of transformation, perseverance, letting go of expectations and limitations and the glory and grace that exists in my journey.

SECTION

Winter – Survival,
Leveraging Resources,
Reorganize

Winter – Survival, Leveraging Resources, Reorganize

IN WINTER, MAGIC IS in the air. It's time to put everything together you have learned and make your plans. The night sky is the brightest during winter. Water crystalizes and comes together. Crystallization signifies the manifestation and coming together of ideas and actions.

5.1 Success Planning

There is so much that I want to do and so much that I want to manifest. I feel like the first half of my life was spent surviving and healing. Now that I have some survival skills and have done a lot of healing, I feel driven to achieve what I was put on this earth for. I feel the need to bring my ideas and dreams to fruition. My greatest fear in life has always been that I won't be able to fulfill my full potential in this lifetime by letting fear drive my actions.

As a Gemini, ideas pop like popcorn in my head. Sometimes they are hard to hold onto and often create a distraction and a lack of focus. Writing this book and getting to the point that you're reading it has been a challenge and a struggle. I sit down, and before I can finish one paragraph, my mind starts to jump around. It goes to other projects and business models, laundry, bills, the meaning of life, home remodeling ideas, the health of my dogs, and much more. The topics are endless.

Another challenge for me is consistency. Related to my popcorn mind, my inconsistency is born of boredom, impatience, and insecurity. At times, I lack the discipline necessary to bring things to a conclusion. I'm a really good starter. I need to work on my finishes.

Far too many of my clients struggle with having no idea of what they want to do. They know and feel in their bones that they want to do something, something bigger, but do not have a clue where to begin.

Starting with a blank page can be intimidating. My belief, however, is that this can be an exciting time. At this stage, there is the freedom to explore ideas without barriers or expectations. You get to try out new things and explore new territory to see what really interests you. It's a time to play. As Albert Einstein said, "Play is the highest form of research."

Always remember—no decision is permanent. You can change your mind and switch directions whenever you want to. If you started something and it does not feel right to you—abandon it and move on quickly. Don't waste time. Just make sure it's not your fears getting you to quit. You need to balance quickly moving on to something else with the ability to stick through the difficult periods.

The keys to achieving your dreams are:

· Creating a clear vision of what you want to achieve

· Establish habits, routines, and rituals to support you along the way

· Clearly define your why (your motivation)

· Developing an action plan to get you there

· Setting up accountability checkpoints along the way

· And continuing to bust through self-doubt (you've already started this work)

5.2 Getting Clear

> "The more clarity you achieve, the more you will find that the universe is on your side, supporting your thoughts and intentions.
> Therefore, focus on clarity, not getting results. The results will come according to their own rhythm and timing."—Deepak Chopra

A coach's first tool in their tool bag is to try to get their client to verbally articulate what they want. Getting clarity is a very important part of elevating your life, so we are going to spend some time here, so you have the tools you need to create a clear picture of what you want. Whether it be what goals and aspirations you want to achieve, behaviors you would like to embody, the feelings you would like to have, or who you want to have in your life, getting clarity on what that *looks* and *feels* like is the first vital step.

I believe that we all possess a deep knowing of the direction we want and need to travel. It's those desires that relentlessly keep coming up even if we systematically keep pushing them away. We convince ourselves that it will be too hard or impossible to achieve. We swat away the whispers of our own intuition with fear and perceived logic of why it can never be attained. We let the louder voices of those around us drown out our own inner voice. The fact is every idea followed leads you down the path to the next thing and the next thing and the next thing. That's how this clarity thing works. It comes from action, not sitting around waiting for it to show up.

There are dozens of areas that a client may want to focus on. Even so, the initial focus must be on the area that will make the most impact to improve the quality of their life. It is critical to focus on what one wants *more* of in their life, not less. Then rinse and repeat for the additional improvements they have identified.

I recognize, for some, it's harder to verbalize what they want. Clients often come to see me precisely because they do not know what they want and need help figuring it out. With this set of clients, it is usually the inertia and lack of clarity that is the *exact* problem. These folks feel the drain and frustration of uncertainty. They know that they *need* something but don't know what that something is. They continue on autopilot until they can unpack this information. Being unclear is anxiety-producing.

When you begin to get serious about improving your life, developing a clear picture of what you want your life to look like is imperative. You will have a hard time making progress toward achieving your goals if the destination is shrouded in fog.

Clarity washes away uncertainty. The first step in achieving what you want is to define what it is you desire. You need to excavate and explore what your dreams are—or have been. Create a definition around what those things are that you want in your life and why.

There are three keys to ensure success. Do not limit your thinking. Big goals and dreams are achieved by thinking big. The second key is to do what feels right to you. There are multiple exercises and recommendations in this section. We all have different personalities and styles. Do the activities that work for you.

Finally, don't fall into the trap of getting too attached to a specific outcome. Create details and specificity around what you want, and then be open to the dream changing. As you embark on your journey, you'll be exposed to new things. You don't want to be stuck with an immovable dream. The initial concept of your dream and the ultimate manifestation of your dream will inevitably change. You may radically shift your goals as you start to get exposed to new ways of thinking and doing. This is not only okay but a necessary part of the process. If you get too attached to an outcome, you will not be able to see the beauty of the path you are traveling.

I now have a clear idea of how I want my life to unfold in the next 3-5 years. Even knowing this, I accept the fact that what will transpire in my life might be quite different. Having developed a clear objective allows me to focus my actions in a precise way, rather than being distracted and scattered in my actions, with a lot of tasks left undone. When I feel pulled in many different directions, I am unproductive and tend to shut down. Focusing on just a few projects or areas at a time is what fits my personality type best due to my tendency to get overwhelmed.

My journey to clarity has been a winding road. In my 40s, one of the actions that I took, being the good corporate employee that I was, was to direct my passion for leadership to enrolling in a Ph.D. program in organizational psychology. Spoiler alert, I did *not* receive my Ph.D. I couldn't get past the statistics. But that's another story. This is an example of following one impulse to be exposed to the next thing. During a full day of Saturday class, guest speakers introduced the class to an organization dedicated to advancing coaching as a profession, International Coach Federation (ICF). Up until that point, I had no idea that this was a viable professional option. Ultimately, I learned more about the profession, researched, and eventually found a program to become certified.

Being the only certified coach in the organization gave me a distinct calling card, and I was excited to put my newfound knowledge to good use in a corporate environment where, in my opinion, true coaching at all levels is imperative but sorely missing. I found my outlet by leading a women's empowerment group for five years. I began creating personal and professional development programs and presentations.

A side-hustle business was born. I began posting on social media, where I could flex and practice my writing skills. Without a doubt, my enrollment in the Ph.D. program led me to the field of coaching and my passion for writing. There is no straight line from Organizational Psychology to writing. But by following the whispers and placing myself in certain circumstances, I was able to arrive here, where I am today, with a clear picture of how I want my life to unfold.

During my journey to clarity, I learned several critical lessons. The first lesson is that time is not infinite. It's not too early, and it's never too late to begin the journey of discovery. Your inner voice doesn't begin at a certain age and doesn't go silent after a period of time. We are here on this planet and occupy this lifetime for a finite period. Make the most of your experience here. The sooner you begin letting your inner voice have a place in guiding you to clarity, the better your experience will be.

Lesson number two is that the journey never ends, and there is no absolute destination. When I read these words years from now, I will be able to tell you how my vision for my life changed over time. I will be able to show you that by choosing a path and listening to my intuitive whispers, I, perhaps, ended up somewhere very different. The important thing to realize is it doesn't matter the destination; it matters that you're moving forward along the journey.

Lesson three is your inner voice will place you on the right path. If you listen. My inner voice has always told me to write. But I pushed that voice away. I justified my lack of action by thinking I was too busy and too stressed; who am I to write? I have nothing interesting to say; I'm not educated in literature or writing. It's too late; it's too early in my life. The list goes on. And none of that really matters. I should have listened to that voice all those years ago. The endless inventory of journals and notebooks I possess should have also been a clue.

Lesson four is to pay attention to the human guides put on your path. All along my journey, there have been dozens, maybe hundreds of human guides who have made subtle (and sometimes not so subtle) suggestions about the action I should take. A friend of mine introduced me to the Ph.D. program that we began together. She stopped after one course, but I kept going for a time until I received the message I was there to receive. I followed a human guide who introduced me to their publisher and collaborative writing opportunities. This led me to be a bestselling author and a path for publishing this book.

The fifth, and maybe the most important lesson, is that action will bring clarity. You won't get closer to determining what you want to achieve by thinking about it. I've tried. You must act. Then act again. Take one small step in the direction you desire. Then another small step. Because once you allow your inner voice to be heard, *action* is required. Follow the voice because the more action you take, the clearer your path will become. You will find it harder and harder to ignore your inner voice once your spirit gets invigorated by action.

Where do you fall in the spectrum of defining what it is you desire in your life?

· **Clueless:** "I have no idea what I want to do, but I know I want to do *something*."

· **Turn my idea into reality:** "I think I know what I want, but I don't know how to get started."

· **Information/Inspiration Overload:** "I have too many ideas. I don't know where to focus my energy."

· **Amp up the Volume:** "I'm on my way. I need help to turn up the volume."

If you are clueless—just get started. Progress over perfection. Test, explore, and have fun. Give yourself permission to dream and to play. Even if you are dripping with kids or overcome with other obligations, every small action taken consistently gets you closer.

Journal and revisit these statements as often as you need to develop a little more specificity around your dreams. Your answers may change over time.

If there was nothing in my way, I would ...

I want to be known for ...

I follow or admire/emulate _____ because they ...

Other actions to take to if you truly don't know what it is you want to achieve.

· Declutter. How can you get clear in your mind if the space around you is cluttered? My Gemini mind tells me, "If I can just get organized, I can make progress on my goals." I have a tendency toward clutter—books, notebooks, and office supplies are my weakness. I need to frequently purge things that are no longer needed and organize my desk on a weekly basis because I'm like a tornado with the stuff. Clutter steals energy. It's a distraction. Clear your space, and you'll be able to clear your mind.

· Sleep. Make sure you are prioritizing sleep. Chronic exhaustion leads to a lack of focus, leaving you unable to develop a clear picture of where you want your life to go.

· Nature. Uncomplicated, refreshing, and nourishing. Being out in nature will bring you back to life. It will give you inspiration or, at the very least, allow you to clear your head.

· Take a walk. No music, no books on audio—just you and your brain (maybe a dog on a leash). Get some alone time with yourself outside of your normal setting. I know when I go for a brisk walk without distraction, my brain is the most creative and inspired. Write down thoughts and ideas that come to you.

· Meditation. A little bit of meditation in your life is a game changer. Meditation slows the thought patterns and the information loops you have going on. It allows you to witness the thoughts you have in a non-judgmental way.

· Eat the right foods. When your brain is all hopped up on sugars and carbs, it affects the way your brain functions. Maintaining a healthy body is not about the size of your bum; it's about the overall functionality of your body, including your brain. Your brain does not work as effectively when it's "under the influence" of toxic elements.

· Talk to someone and get a coach. A good coach will ask you the right questions and can lead you down the path of ideas and concepts you should consider and identify what may be holding you back. The coach will uncover hidden beliefs by asking the right series of thought-provoking questions. You might have some hidden beliefs about the way life should be that are holding you back. Talking through these things with a coach can be super effective in setting you on the path of your choosing.

· Journal. Get in touch with your own thoughts by writing them down—like coaching, but without the intuitive questioning part. Write what's on your mind. When thoughts are swirling around in your head, and you are not getting them out on paper or verbally, they go unchallenged. We need to challenge the programming that has been embedded in our minds for years and decades.

· Start with the outcome. I know you don't know what your next steps are or what you want to achieve. An effective exercise is to do some stream-of-consciousness writing. Give yourself some space and private time to describe the life of your dreams in five years. Describe your ideal life with as much specificity as possible. Describe how you *feel*. Do you feel loved, warm, safe, happy, and grateful? The truth is when we want to *do* something or design our lives, truly, what we are after is a *feeling*.

· Have fun and explore. Really, this is my favorite thing. You have the absolute freedom to experiment and have fun and explore opportunities. Make this a fun activity. Try different things. When something doesn't feel right, you have no skin in the game. Just move on to the next thing.

When you need help turning your idea into reality, you have a clear idea of what you want to achieve, but other things are getting in your way. Obligations, like just making ends meet, surpass acting on your goals and dreams. If you've prioritized survival over your dreams, I want you to understand that you don't have to choose either/or—survival or your dreams. The smallest action towards your dreams will compound over time. Small actions add up. Over time and with consistency, you will see these dreams materialize.

- You may have a couple of children hanging off you, running from one activity to the next, taking care of parents, and working long hours. You don't have one single moment to yourself. When you have a moment to breathe, you're exhausted, and you just want to melt into the sofa. Now that you're getting better sleep, look for small pockets of time where you can fit in some quality dedicated, and focused time. Can you wake up 15-30 minutes earlier before the bustle of the day begins? Can you find time on the weekends? Fifteen to thirty minutes each day of the week adds up to two and a half hours a week. Add in another hour or two from the weekend, and you have some significant time to put into your passion project.

- Identify your golden hours. I'm best in the morning, with higher energy and more creativity. Time and time again, I have proven to myself that I am unable to be effective after a long workday. No matter how dedicated and confident I am, the fatigue and stress of the day render me ineffective for productive work on my personal dreams at night. As the day goes on, the excuses and the justifications mount. If you have more energy at night, this may be your optimal time to dedicate to your goals.

- There may be some things you can take off your plate. Take an honest inventory of what's taking up your time. What things are you doing because you're the only one who can do them correctly? What can you delegate? What can you outsource? What can you eliminate because it's not providing you any value in your life?

· Consider your priorities. How will your priorities change two, four, or six years from now? Life is always changing, along with schedules and circumstances. Obligations go away, and others may come in their place. It will be beneficial to take some time to look at your life in the coming years. Are children going to school more often or leaving the nest? Your life will change over the next few years. There will be a time when you're obligations change. Design your plans accordingly.

If you suffer from information or inspiration overload, you can relate to my Gemini mind of having too many ideas. There are a lot of things I want to do and a lot of things I want to create. Ideas and inspiration are infinite. The problem is I get overwhelmed. When I'm in a state of overload, every little thing seems much more complicated. Often, I get stuck because I don't know where to start. And when I do start, I get distracted by other ideas.

Here are some ways to start getting focused on where to direct your energy:

· Is your fear the reason you can't focus? Having too much that you want to do can be a tactic used to keep playing small by never putting yourself out there in a real way. You may have a fear of success, so you put up obstacles to keep you from achieving your goals. Explore your thoughts and feelings around success and failure.

· Be strategic—where do you see yourself in five years? I keep asking versions of this question throughout the workbook. It's so important to understand where you see yourself in the future. If a project or idea doesn't get you closer to this ideal state, you may want to reconsider its importance. If it doesn't give you a skill or put you in contact with a critical network of people, it may not be worth doing at this time. I'm not saying to give up something you're passionate about. If it nags at you and you can't get rid of the idea, you should absolutely explore it. However, if this idea is just on your long list of things to do, a half-finished project that makes you feel bad about yourself, or something you know you'll never get around to crossing off your list, it's time to remove it from your list.

· Give yourself some distance to gain perspective—sometimes, you just need a break and a little distance to get clear. You may have been in a state of being overwhelmed for way too long that you can't see the forest for the trees. Take the weekend or the week off. When you come back to it, apply the techniques in this section to get a fresh start. Give yourself permission to delay or scrap some ideas. This is your life, your dreams, and you get to create the life you want to live. Every second of every day, you get to choose. Then you get to choose again, change your mind, or modify your approach. If something is not bringing you joy, reassess. Remember that hard work on a project is not joyful all the time, but if the idea of the finished product doesn't bring you joy, reconsider its position on your list.

· Is it *your* dream you're trying to bring to life, or is it someone else's? Simply ask yourself why you want to achieve this goal. If the answer is solely to satisfy someone else, it's time to reconsider its placement on your list.

You have a dream and it's time to accelerate and amp up the volume. I have a dream. of setting off on my entrepreneurial journey without the comfort of the corporate paycheck. Scary!! I know. But I know that I can be more effective and deliver more of what I'm good at if I'm able to do this full-time. However, with a Gemini brain like mine, I get distracted by all my "great" ideas and butterflies, dogs barking, and laundry. I also have the dream to dollar for dollar replace my corporate income. Yikes. But why not? Really, there is no reason I can't make this happen. If you're in a similar situation where it's time to make some significant progress, it is time for you to really set some specific and significant goals. It's time to see some progress in your focused area.

· If you're ready to amp up the volume of making your dreams happen, you must ensure that your foundation is cared for. You'll need the energy. Ensure your mental capabilities are supported through mental wellness.

· Don't minimize your dreams. Big thinking precedes your big dreams coming true. Do not play small.

· Track your time. If you want to ensure you are being productive with your time, see where your time goes. Find pockets of time to dedicate to your growth and success. Identify what you are committed to over the next month. Get rid of unnecessary meetings or activities.

· Watch for burnout. You will be no good to anyone if you are burned out. Take breaks. Breaks will allow your brain and body to recharge to continue your path.

· Set goals and deadlines for yourself. Be your own project manager. Understand your timelines and what needs to be done, and when. Identify the tasks that are quick to complete and get them out of the way so you can focus on the items that take more energy and creativity.

· Be accountable. If you blow past your deadlines—because, well, who's impacted beside you and your dreams—it's time you find an accountability partner. Tell a friend or a colleague what you are trying to achieve. Give them permission to check in on you. Or get yourself a coach.

· Get over the myth of multitasking. Many high achievers take a lot of pride in being able to do multiple things at once. This is a fallacy. You are only physically able to do one thing at a time. Give up your multitasking badge of honor.

· Prioritize *done* over perfection. As Anne Lamott says, she focuses on completing the "shitty first draft" of any book that she writes. But this isn't just for writing. It can be said of a lot of things. Just get it out of your head and onto paper (or screen, or wherever your dream or goal resides). Get something done and give yourself permission *not* to be perfect.

5.3 Habits

> "How you start your day is how you live your day. How you live your day is how you live your life."—Louise Hay

We are what we repeatedly do. Strong habits are the building blocks for success and reaching goals. Goal achievement requires some structure, even if you're an extremely spontaneous person. Think of developing habits, routines and rituals as aligning your most important work with how and when you're most effective. It's the establishment of systems to keep you moving toward your goals.

Without established habits, routines, and rituals, I am rendered unproductive and lost. I feel aimless and unmotivated. Habits provide a sort of grounding, an ability to know what to expect of yourself and a structure that gives you a sense that you're moving in the right direction. If I spend a day without some of my powerful routines, I feel like I've lost valuable time. I let slip away the opportunity that I might have had to make progress on my dreams. Getting lost in a binge-fest on a regular basis is not very productive. Listen, I'm not telling you to not binge. Binging on shows has its place, but for me, I need to dedicate binge time during the least mentally and physically productive times of my day—the early to late evening. My high-quality thinking of the day is over by this time. If I feel like it, I will binge then. If I start binging in the morning, it can go all day. Next thing you know, its dinner time, and you haven't even taken a shower yet, much less made progress on your goals.

Tips for creating habits:

· Start small. Don't plan to dedicate eight hours that first day to a project when you haven't even put in 30 minutes a day. Start doing just one small task a day for one week, and you'll increase your chances of success.

· Once you've nailed one good habit, start adding other actions to your day. Slowly. If you ever start to feel overwhelmed, step back a little. Give yourself the space and the time to get it right.

· Put triggers to remind you what you need to do. Putting your running shoes by the door or prepping your ingredients for your morning green drink the night before will trigger you to act.

· Find someone to hold you accountable. Tell someone you trust about your plans. And very importantly, give them permission to hold you accountable. Plan to check in weekly.

· Do research—who is doing what you're doing? Watch what they do, talk to them, follow them. What habits have they incorporated to be successful?

· Document it. Write down your morning routine. Create a schedule and invest in a planner. Create a routine where every morning, for ten minutes, you dedicate time to writing down what your day is going to look like. Set yourself up for success by knowing when you are at your most focused.

If you are a morning person, but you decide that you are going to work out in the evening, you might be setting yourself up to be disappointed. If you are at your most alert and active in the evening but want to write your novel in the morning, you may be setting yourself up for failure.

· Stop waiting for "motivation" to show up. Rarely do I feel like writing. To me, writing can be uncomfortable. It's a time full of vulnerability and self-doubt. I often feel like quitting after ten minutes. Or even worse, I start distracting myself with social media or other forms of mindlessness. And when the restlessness gets bad, I start to think about all the things I need to do around the house. Just start, keep going, and redirect your mind when it starts to go a little crazy.

· Don't forget to put self-care in the bucket of habits you need to create. If you're on the hamster wheel of obligation, this one's for you. You need to put some meditation, exercise, journaling, reading, and baths on your list. You need to be able to recharge and if you have trouble allowing yourself this time, schedule it. Do whatever you need to do to make yourself feel more like you.

5.4 Create a Vision and Action Plan

"Vision without action is merely a dream.
Action without vision just passes time.

> Vision and action can change the world."
> —Joel A Barker

Creating a vision for your life will help you overcome resistance. If your definition of success is random thoughts in your head without specificity, you can become overwhelmed by the perceived obstacles. Write it out, identify any barriers then create a plan to overcome them.

Once you have a clear vision and the steps needed to achieve your goals, it will motivate you to act. The vision that you create for your life should be audacious with no limitations. Taking the extra step to align your values with your vision will prime you for success. When your goals are not tied to a bigger meaning it allows you to easily disregard and deprioritize them.

Your vision should look three to five years out. It should be aspirational and even a bit scary. Don't assign logic when creating your vision. Don't think you don't have the money, time, or resources to make it happen. None of that matters in this vision.

In your journal, use this simple exercise to align your values with your vision:

What I want to do:

How I want to feel:

Why I want to do it:

Where I want to do it:

Put it all tougher to create a five-year vision:

Example: "By the year 2028 I will …

Do not skip this step. It begins to create a blueprint for your future and what you want to achieve. You wouldn't build a house without a blueprint. You need to have a design of what you want your life to look like, or your actions and your goals will be misaligned. Doing this will also take you off autopilot. You will begin to live your life intentionally instead of randomly. This exercise will also allow you to make decisions on the actions you want to take in the future. Will the action you take bring you closer to your vision? If not, that action either needs to be reprioritized in your life, or you need to evaluate if your vision still aligns with your values.

Create Your Action Plan

Take your five-year vision and make sure that you're dreaming big. Don't limit yourself. Make sure your vision incorporates how you want to feel and why your goal is important to you.

It will take time to manifest your vision. It will also take attention and intention. The next step to making your vision a reality is to visualize where you need to be in time increments. To make your five-year vision a reality, where will you need to be in three years? In one year?

You have now created a meaningful roadmap to achieve your dream. One final step is to set up to ensure success is setting up a system of accountability to keep you reaching for your goals.

Your accountability partner can be someone in your tribe who has similar goals and aspirations. A coach can be a sounding board for your vision, help review your plan, giving you the perspective of someone who doesn't have any emotional ties. The important thing is to find someone who is objective and who doesn't have any skin in the game. People who care for you deeply can potentially project their fears onto you. They also may let you "off the hook" if you complain to them about how hard the journey is. They'll be too sympathetic. Find a person who will be compassionately firm with you and give you the tough love you need.

People who create systems of accountability in their lives accelerate their performance. An accountability partner or coach will help you to define what success looks like and will keep you engaged in the process, even during times when you feel like giving up. Especially those times.

TIME WITH THE COACH:

Where are you at on the clarity scale?

What *immediate* actions are you ready to take?

Try the following exercises if you're still struggling to gain clarity.

Daily Journaling Exercise #1:

Find a simple notebook. Open the notebook where you have a blank sheet of paper on the left side of the page while also seeing a blank page on the right side.

On the top of the left page, write **IF in (the year 3 years from now)**. On the top of the right page, write **THEN today (today's date) I must...**

On your **IF** page, write what your life will look like in three years if you achieve the goals you want to achieve. Write with as much detail as possible. How does your day start? Who are you with? How do you look physically? What house are you in, and in what geographic area? What do you do first? Second? Are you working? What work are you doing? How do you live your day? What happens throughout the day and into the evening? How does your day end? You're writing your dream life; how do you imagine living your day?

Next, on the **THEN** page, write what you must do today to support and achieve your dream day. If your dream is to be physically stronger and to own your own business, *then* today, you need to go to the gym and conduct entrepreneurial or industry-specific research.

Continue with your **IF/THEN** pages to sustain your motivation and belief that you'll be able to take the necessary action to get you to where you want to be.

Daily Journaling Exercise #2:

If you are having a difficult time narrowing your focus, try this technique to reduce your desires down to a succinct list. The exercise is called "21 Things."

When we want to accomplish a lot of things, we have a hard time knowing where our focus should go. In this exercise, you will write all the things that you want to do or accomplish. These are the things you've been thinking about doing; you may have some half-finished activities. It's time to prioritize your attention by reducing the list, so you're able to focus on completing or achieving what is most important to you.

The list can contain projects that you want to work on around the home, job or career aspirations, health-related activities, family, and friend-related activities—anything that you would like to make a priority in your life. Anything that you would like to have more of right now.

You'll do this exercise over the course of six days. On the first day, you'll write out 21 things that you want to have or do. Let this be almost a stream of consciousness. Don't overanalyze the items. Don't think about feasibility or probability. Just write out the 21 things. You may find you'll only come up with 15. But keep thinking and make a complete list of 21.

On day two, you will re-write the list. This time, you'll reduce the list by three. Your list will now have "18 Things" you want to accomplish. Make sure you don't just cross out three of the times. You may find that you thought of something else you want to add to the list. But this time, you can only write 18 things. When you're writing out your 18, add a little clarity or specificity to some of the items.

You'll continue this exercise in the same manner for four more days, each day writing three items fewer. At the end of the six days, you'll have the three items that you want to work on in the immediate future to bring to fruition. Journal about why these three things remained on the list. Why are they so important to you? What feelings do you have about the final three?

YOUR SUCCESS MEDITATION

ESSENTIAL OILS

The following essential oils are associated with success. Cinnamon signifies success. Peppermint attracts prosperity. Patchouli attracts money, and bergamot brings good luck in business.

YOUR SUCCESS MANTRA

I am destined to succeed

YOUR SUCCESS BREATHING TECHNIQUE

Use the following breathing technique to promote increased brain functionality while supporting the reduction of negative emotions. Inhale slowly to the count of four. Hold the breath for a count of seven. Exhale to the count of eight. Repeat this technique five times prior to entering your success meditation.

YOUR SUCCESS MEDITATION

Find a quiet place where you won't be disturbed. After completing the breathing technique provided, do a complete body scan (see Honor Your Story Meditation) to release all the tension you've built up.

Say your success mantra silently to yourself: I am destined to succeed.

Success is demonstrated by the emotions that you feel, not the things you have. Feel the feelings of enthusiasm. When you are successful, you are excited to be alive. Sit with the feelings of enthusiasm. Where in your body do you feel the sensation of enthusiasm?

Feel the feelings of confidence. Sit with the feelings of confidence, knowing that you have achieved so much personal growth. You've come a long way, and you have a lot to be confident about. Where in your body do you feel the sensation of confidence?

Feel the feelings of belief. Sit with the feelings of having a strong belief system that allows you to believe in your dreams and your ability to achieve them. Where in your body do you feel the sensation of belief?

Feeling the feelings of being focused. Sit with the feelings of being able to focus on yourself and your dreams. Both you and your dreams are important. Where in your body do you feel the sensation of focus?

Feel the feelings of having peace of mind. Sit with the feelings of not having to worry about the future or anything else. You are enveloped by peace. Where in your body do you feel the sensation of peace?

Feel the feelings of celebration. Sit with the feelings of being able to celebrate. It's okay to celebrate yourself. Where in your body do you feel the sensation of celebration?

Sit as long as you need to in this meditation. Feel the most dominant feelings of success throughout your body and even to your bones.

As you return to room awareness, journal any thoughts or feelings that came up for you during this meditation. Was it easy or hard to feel the feelings of success?

A WALK-THROUGH NATURE

JOSHUA TREE'S CONTRAST

A week in Palm Springs was exactly what my spirit needed when my dear sister-in-law offered a retreat exactly one year after the pandemic lockdown began. A week of communing with nature was planned, but I knew what was really calling my name. I longed for the sacred grandeur of Joshua Tree National Park.

As a person who is recharged by the water, Joshua Tree's desert landscape's beckoning resides deep in my soul. If you've been, you know. You feel it. It is an expanse of rock formations, big skies, and desert plants and trees. There is nothing to do in Joshua Tree except *feel* Joshua Tree. It is devoid of light pollution, noise pollution, cell phone signals, and all other forms of urban life. As it strips away all the modern world's trappings, it leaves your soul stripped of all that is unnecessary.

My ever-accommodating sister-in-law fell prey to my desire to chase sunrises and sunsets during our trip. One morning we woke at three a.m. to set out on our journey. Cameras and snacks packed, we raced to a spot I had visited before. Barker Dam had been ravaged by California's drought since my last visit. The water I was expecting was now a dry bed of rock and brush.

But Joshua Tree always surprises me. It reveals constant wonder and contrast, strength, and beauty. That morning I was gifted by the sight of a blanket of snow on the desert floor. Joshua Tree averages one inch of snow per year. Eighty percent of the year, the sun radiates through the expansive National Park. So, I was indeed amazed on this early morning by the layer of fresh powder. I couldn't get over the contradictory nature of this magical place and was grateful for our luck to be able to witness this transformative miracle of snow in the Mojave Desert.

I parked the car, and we began our walk on the Barker Dam trail. It was an easy trail covered in fresh snow, clinging to the untouched trail and ancient rocks. We saw rare pops of color, desert holly of red, green, and white, presented like a late Christmas gift. The cacti were covered in snow and ice. Snowcapped mountains in the distance were dusted with the pink sunrise. We passed the empty dam and found ourselves in a field of Joshua Trees.

The serenity came down upon me from the sky, washing over me. There was nothing, and there was everything. We were placed on the altar of Mother Nature.

Joshua Tree's conditions are unyielding. Walking through the park, I heard the slight sound of running water. Knowing that the dam was dry, it took me a few minutes to realize that the snow was melting and dripping from the trees so rapidly it sounded like the drizzle of rain in the distance. The transformation of the desert landscape can be quick, and by the time we exited the park a few hours later, the snow was a memory captured in my mind, my spirit, and my camera.

Joshua Tree's spiritual message is one of perseverance with the existence of seemingly contrasting conditions. When all is stripped away, magic and beauty can still exist. When all that is unnecessary gets washed away, this is the place where true healing and transformation occur. Joshua Tree reminds us that this is a *both/and* world, not *either/or*. There can be harsh conditions and beauty. There can be pain and joy. There can be sickness and healing. When one season ends, another begins. Transformation is guaranteed while coexisting with steadiness and grounding found in nature.

At the visitors' center, I picked up a plaque that read, "Nature is Cheaper than Therapy." Let nature assist you in healing your mind, body, and spirit. She's there waiting for you, longing for you to use Her in that way.

SECTION Six

The Journey Never Ends

The Journey Never Ends

YOU'RE NEARING THE END of this book, but your story doesn't end here. I've given you a lifetime of practices to come back to over and over. Just as in nature, there are always additional places to explore, learn, grow, and evolve.

Along the way, you've been identifying areas that are on your watch list. These are the things that, as you continue your journey, you will need to come back to and evaluate your mindset and do the exercises again to make sure these areas don't undermine your success.

You are transforming yourself back into the person you were born to be—strong, purposeful, confident, and joyful. You will come to realize, more and more every day, that you are here to stay. You will never again fade into the background or limit yourself unnecessarily.

6.1 Continue the Momentum

Commit to yourself to never stop your evolution. It's vital you take advantage of those times when you are being super productive. If you're feeling it, if you're in the groove, don't let that feeling go to waste. You have the power to create your best life. You now have the tools and resources to make the journey a reality.

Momentum can continue when you are able to celebrate all that you've accomplished. Be shamelessly proud of how far you've come. Continue to do little things every day that elevate your experience on this earth. But most importantly, give yourself grace. The work of healing and achieving our own personal best is not an easy path. Not everyone decides to take that journey. You, however, have been called to take that journey. You have come this far and are reading these words because you decided to embark on this incredibly difficult but rewarding expedition.

6.2 Rebounding

You have all the tools you need here to get back on track when you falter. And you will falter. We all get off track. Life happens to everyone. As we learn more about ourselves and grow, other lessons or triggers will stop progress. Recognize that this is normal and it's how the universe works. As you evolve and heal and return to your true nature, you will be triggered by people, fears, and life's circumstances.

You will be required to sometimes take a step back and reassess.

Forgive yourself for not being perfect in execution. Because you are not. Nobody is. You are perfectly imperfect.

If life has set you back for whatever reason, this is the time to ensure you are focusing on self-care and wellness. It's time to go back to the *Foundation* section of the book and make sure you are taking care of your physical health. This is the fastest way to get back on track.

Reinforce your connections if you need support. Nothing is more healing than true friendships. If you need mental health support, reach out to a professional and get the help you need. There is absolutely no shame. We need to continue to talk about mental wellness and encourage one another to take advantage of therapy and other available services. There is no reason to suffer alone.

We all fall down, fall away, lose our balance, and lose our momentum. It's going to happen. Expect it. You need to give yourself grace and time to deal with the things in life that inevitably come up and throw us off track.

Adjust your perspective and ask yourself if the change you're going through is a lesson that you need to learn. Has something become a pattern? Unlearned lessons keep showing up in interesting and challenging ways. The universe is trying to tell you something. Be still and listen. Maybe it's trying to tell you that you need a change in direction; maybe you need to change your priorities and find joy in your life. Perhaps you need to learn how to deal with a particular situation, challenge, or person. And maybe it's trying to tell you that you need some rest, that you've been pushing too hard for too long.

Find your balance, then rebound to your set point.

TIME WITH THE COACH

What are some of your triggers that you need to watch out for?

Have you incorporated the tools provided here: meditation, breathwork, and journaling into your life?

What area(s) are on your watch list?

What activities do you need to reincorporate into your life?

Rebound in nature. Choose one of these inspiring and restorative activities to do when you need to be rejuvenated:

· Create a ritual to celebrate each new season. Each season brings change that is mirrored in our own lives. Reflect on what the new season means to you and the gifts it can bring. Observe the changes you see. Practice gratitude and honor mother earth for her resilience.

· Sleep outside. Whether you're a camper or take a nap on your front porch, there is something about sleeping outside that separates you from the connected world and brings you to a primal state of being.

- Ground yourself in nature. Walk barefoot on the earth. One of my favorite ways to do this is to water the grass barefoot. I imagine roots from my feet planting themselves into the ground. It provides me comfort when I'm feeling overwhelmed and anxious.

- Plan your next vacation to a national park. These magnificent places are protected for a reason. The expanse and beauty that you can witness in a national park are life changing.

- Plant a garden. If you don't have room, plant an indoor herb garden. Get your hands in the dirt and watch seeds bust through with their little green stems and leaves. It's endlessly exciting, to me at least, to see the daily new growth and transformation of something that you planted.

- Watch a sunrise or a sunset. Watching the sun make its first appearance of the day or watching it take its last bow of the day as it lights up the sky and the earth brings you closer to source energy.

- Intentionally experience nature with all your senses. Pay attention to the sights, the sounds, the smells, the touch, and even the taste of what nature gives to us.

- Do something creative out in nature. My favorite is photography. But you can paint, draw, or play music out in nature. A great way to thank Mother Nature is by creating with her.

- Enjoy the night sky. If you can go to a spot where there is less "light pollution," you will be able to see the dimensions of the night sky that you couldn't before. The vastness of the universe can be most felt looking at the night sky.

· Create altars in nature. Selecting items from nature to create an homage or mandala-type image honors all parts of nature, even those parts that are being shed. Check out the book *Morning Altars* by Day Schildkret. His approach to creating rituals and altars out of items you find in nature is so unique.

Never forget that nature is a resource that is always available to you. When you feel separated from your own true nature, step outside and experience the magic Mother Nature has to offer. She's there to remind you of your place in this world.

About the Author

Janet Zavala is a bestselling author, coach and nature enthusiast who is passionate about making proven self-empowerment techniques accessible to a greater number of people. Her unique style incorporates traditional coaching techniques with the healing power of nature to help clients dig deeper into all aspects of their lives—mind, body, and spirit—and see where they are experiencing difficulties, identify the source of what's keeping them stuck, and develop a plan to get them where they need to be.

Working in corporate America for over 30 years, Janet observed the everyday worker who needs the support quality coaching can provide. When people are struggling at work, it's rarely about the work itself. The barriers are internal. First, Janet started coaching employees who reported to her, then began coaching peers and other staff members while building a thriving coaching practice. She witnessed well-crafted questions, and supportive conversations helped not only improve the confidence of her clients but also exponentially helped them in their career and life.

Wanting to make coaching techniques more accessible has been her driving force.

Leveraging her skills in public speaking, creating, and delivering original content, and group coaching programs, she began leading a women's empowerment group. Providing thought leadership and strategic guidance in the development of cohesive and comprehensive events and activities focused on personal and professional development, she delivered hundreds of staff members in over 30 events.

In her spare time, she enjoys being out in nature, observing and learning about the parallel between the transformation of plants and flowers from hikes while growing and nurturing own her garden. No longer a "black thumb," she simply realized that paying more attention to what the plants require allows them to thrive. Taking the right action to allow them to have the proper sunlight, space to grow, water, and other nutrients, so closely aligns with what we need, as humans, to thrive. As an amateur nature photographer, she enjoys documenting nature's transformation. Her love of coaching and wonder of nature is where much of the inspiration for this book has been derived

She finds enrichment in activities like reading, writing, photography, and gardening and is grounded in her daily meditation practice. She has been in a book club for nearly 15 years with her dearest friends and constantly seeks out new courses, ideologies, and sources of information to improve her personal effectiveness and to improve her effectiveness with clients. She is the mother to one human son and two fur-children.

Made in the USA
Las Vegas, NV
16 November 2023